CW00949789

"So many voices out there are ___ themselves to find their purpo___ Rice. I love that about her and t___ the only reliable source for iden___ ___ purpose, and meaning— the Scriptures. With insight and wisdom drawn from the book of Ephesians, Sarah speaks to matters every woman has to work through and make sense of—empowerment, belonging, purpose, identity and conflict."

Nancy Guthrie, Bible teacher and author of *I'm Praying for You* and *Even Better Than Eden*

"Sarah traces a beautiful theology of womanhood, one rightly anchored in union with Christ. She challenged me over and over, in her clear and readable style, particularly reminding me that self is no longer the central project of my life. Sarah is no rookie to the lies of this world, but she is a robust theologian who dissolves these lies powerfully with Christ and his gospel light."

Natalie Brand, Bible teacher and author of *Priscilla, Where Are You?*

"If my mom, wife, daughters or friends are going to read a book on gospel identity, I want it to be by someone who has been gripped by the gospel herself, someone who knows that she (like the rest of us) is imperfect, in need of daily grace, and has learned (and is still learning) to revel in the complete forgiveness and acceptance that God grants in Jesus. Sarah Rice is that someone. Sarah writes with candor, humor and precision, and she makes profoundly important concepts clear and applicable. More importantly, as her pastor I can say that she lives every day in light of the beautiful truths she so winsomely explains. I cannot recommend this book highly enough!"

John Sloan, Senior Pastor, Capshaw Baptist Church, Alabama

"With clarity and winsomeness, Sarah Rice offers her readers a rich, Biblical foundation for understanding what it means to be a woman who is formed by the gospel. This is a wonderful resource for the church!"

Ann Swindell, author of *The Path to Peace* and owner of Writing with Grace

"If you're confused about whether female empowerment is a good thing, or you wonder if you'll ever be good enough or truly feel loved, read this book. After refuting gospel-void lies like *I'm basically good* or *I have to find my unique self*, Sarah shows us how our deepest questions are answered and problems resolved when we are reunited with Jesus Christ—the one making all things new. By clearly applying the gospel to various aspects of womanhood, such as work, physical bodies, friendship, marriage and more, Sarah offers us true freedom and the real basis for our worth."

Shannon Popkin, author of *Shaped by God's Promises* and host of the Live Like It's True Bible Podcast.

Gospel-shaped Womanhood

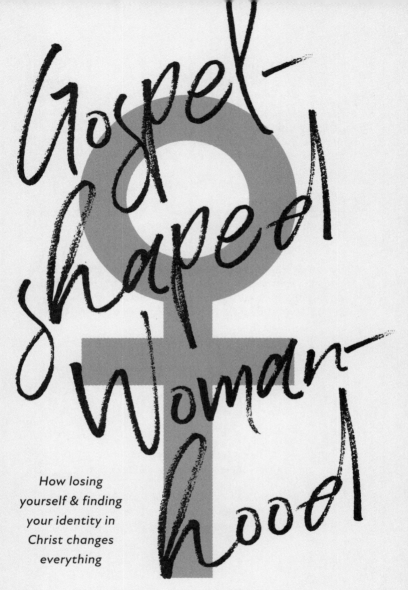

Gospel-shaped Womanhood

How losing yourself & finding your identity in Christ changes everything

SARAH RICE

10 Publishing
a division of 10ofthose.com

British Library Cataloguing in Publication Data

A record for this book is available from the British Library

ISBN: 9781914966880

Designed by Jude May

Printed in Denmark
10Publishing, a division of 10ofthose.com

Unit C, Tomlinson Road, Leyland, PR25 2DY, England
Email: info@10ofthose.com
Website: www.10ofthose.com

3 5 7 10 8 6 4 2

To: Mom

The "Titus 2" older woman in my life,
the one who first taught me to find my identity in Christ,
a gospel-shaped woman through and through.
In love and gratitude, I dedicate this book to you.

Contents

Introduction

Given Not Made

*W*e live in an age where women have both the freedom and the pressure to forge a personal identity. Voices within our individualistic culture tell us it's our right and our responsibility to discover and define who we are. They teach us to look deep within to find our most authentic selves and then pursue a path that keeps us true to that self. In other words, we are living in "find yourself, live your truth, you do you" times—times in which we are (supposedly) free to be whoever we want to be.

But is identity really ours to create? Do self-discovery and self-definition actually bring true freedom and peace? We all desperately want answers to the same questions: *Am I valuable? Wanted? Secure? Truly loved? Does my life have purpose? Do I belong?* The world says we will discover the answers to these questions *within* as we learn to love ourselves while rehearsing the mantra "I am enough." Yet, the world also bombards us with endless advice on how to be *better.* Books, blogs, and videos abound, offering tips and instructions for becoming healthier, happier, more organized, successful, and attractive versions of ourselves. If it's true that identity is self-made, we're left with the constant and heavy burden of trying to measure and validate our "enoughness" by some unknown standard. Could what the world markets as freedom really just enslave us?

In our quest to forge a personal identity, we often define ourselves according to our roles, preferences, family history, relationships, work, physical appearance, and a host of fluctuating factors too unstable to support the weight of our womanhood. If our worth as women is based on what we *do*, what happens when we stop doing that thing, or when we fail to do it well? If our security and sense of acceptance are completely wrapped up in earthly relationships, personal achievement, or a fit and healthy body, what happens when those things are lost? When the sources of a self-made identity are stripped away, we're left empty and hopeless.

But what if we recognized that identity is not ours to create because we didn't self-originate, and so we don't actually belong to ourselves? What if we simply received an identity that sealed our worth, security, belonging, and the love of another forever? What if we confidently knew this identity would grant us permanent rest from striving and enable us to face our brokenness with the sure hope of healing and wholeness? If this identity is really ours, then belonging to another is actually extremely good news!

In a world incessantly pushing us to build our identity on all the wrong things, I wrote *Gospel-Shaped Womanhood* to help women see that identity *in Christ* is the only stable and lasting foundation upon which to build a life. Through his Son, God freely grants sinners a gospel identity powered by *grace*. This is the only identity that gives us eternal rest from striving while also propelling us to live a life of good works.

In his letter to the Ephesian Church, the Apostle Paul outlines the big picture of what it means to be *in Christ* and explains how this identity works itself out practically, not only in God's grand purposes for the cosmos, but also in the details of day-to-day life. Paul's gospel identity so defined him that he forsook every other potential foundation for self, and this reality flows out in his writing. Paul wanted believers to deeply ground themselves in Christ, understanding how their identity in him transforms every aspect of their lives.

The Apostle spends the first three chapters of Ephesians surveying all God has done in Christ. He rejoices in the spiritual blessings lavished on believers, the wonders of salvation, and the stunning mystery of the gospel now revealed. In chapters four through six, Paul gets practical in how these truths impact our daily decisions, work, relationships, and family life. Reflecting the pattern of Ephesians, I've divided the following chapters into two sections to help us see how knowing *who* we are (Part 1) impacts *what* we do (Part 2). In other words, becoming grounded in our identity *in* Christ, shapes and drives our activity *for* Christ in every area of life.

In Part 1, "Gospel-Shaped Identity," we see the scope of all Christ has achieved for us in salvation, and the wonderful benefits of gospel identity. These chapters delve into how, in Christ, women are given the eternal worth, purpose, acceptance, and love, we all so desperately need. We explore how the indwelling Holy Spirit is a woman's only source of power for truly good and hopeful living, and how the gospel reverses the estrangement and alienation caused by sin. At the end of this section, we get into the often-tricky relationship between grace and works for the believer, which is the foundation for all that follows in the second half of the book.

In Part 2, "Gospel-Shaped Activity," we get really practical in how the gospel impacts our work, our friendships, our bodies, and our marriages or singleness as women. These chapters work through what an unshakeable identity in Christ looks like in the everyday—at the work meeting or the play-date, in our interactions at church, when our favorite jeans are suddenly too tight, or when we're wondering how to spend an evening alone. We consider together how being in Christ is good news for every area of life, both in the joys and in the struggles. The final chapter explores how we should view suffering and our role in the world. Drawing on Paul's famous passage about the armor of God, we see how the life of a Christian woman is a life of war—and ultimately victory.

Before you dive in here, commit to read or listen to the entire book of Ephesians in one sitting. This takes about 20 minutes, and it will help prepare your heart and mind for what you will encounter in this book. In addition, to get the most out of *Gospel-Shaped Womanhood*, I recommend not rushing through but taking time to consider the impact of each topic on your heart and life. Each chapter ends with discussion questions to use in a discipleship group, book club, or individually for personal reflection. Reading and discussing the book with other sisters in Christ would be especially helpful, allowing you to encourage one another in remembering your shared identity, while spurring one another to the good works God has prepared for you (Eph. 2:10).

While many factors *shape* and *describe* us as individual women, God alone has the power and authority to *define* us. My prayer is that, as Christian women, we become grounded in the good news that Jesus Christ brings lasting *rest*. In him, we can stop attempting to build an identity and prove our worthiness. He releases us from the endless pressure to be enough. Gospel-shaped women learn to rest and work by the power of grace as we believe this truth: Only the love of God in Christ tells us who we really are and transforms us into who we were made to be.

Part 1:

GOSPEL-SHAPED IDENTITY

1

The Only Good News

What the gospel is and what it isn't

For by grace you have been saved through faith. And this is not your own doing; it is the gift of God, not a result of works, so that no one may boast.
—*Ephesians 2:8–9*

"What is the gospel?" The question seemed basic enough, but she stared at me across the coffee table like a deer caught in headlights. A few moments of awkward silence ensued before she attempted to respond: "Well, I know what the gospel is... I just don't really know how to explain it." I was talking with a fifteen-year-old girl who had recently started seeing me for biblical counseling. The daughter of devout Christian parents, she attended a private Christian school and was at church almost every time the doors opened. But since I never want to assume church attendance means a person is a Christian, I began that session as I begin all early counseling sessions—with lots of questions.

One question I always ask is whether or not the person is a believer in Jesus Christ. If the answer is yes, I follow up by asking her to share her testimony of coming to faith and her understanding of the Christian gospel. What I have found in multiple counseling sessions (and within the church in general) has been both shocking and discouraging: Many women who profess to be Christians are unable to clearly articulate the gospel of Jesus Christ. Even worse, a number of women have placed their trust in a false gospel without even realizing it.

False gospels are proclaimed everywhere we turn—through social media, blogs, best-selling books, and even by some churches—and the scary reality is that they can sound *so* right. They're popular and self-affirming, packaged in punchy clichés that tickle the ears and make us feel warm and fuzzy inside. Many false gospels, particularly here in the West, herald the "good news" of you and me—exhorting us to put our hope in ourselves. At first blush, these messages sound so positive and promising, but they're actually proclaiming self as Savior and Lord rather than Christ. And this is very bad news.

So, what are we to do? With false gospels bombarding us at every turn, how do we know that we're believing the truth? We must turn to the Scriptures to discern what the true gospel is and what it is not. If we are to find our identity in Christ and allow him to shape every part of our lives, we must know his gospel inside and out. We must know it not just intellectually but also experientially. We must rest in it personally, not just nod our agreement. In order to be gospel-shaped women, we must be able to distinguish the authentic gospel from its many sneaky counterfeits, and once we know it, we must root our entire lives deep within it.

No bad news, no good news

A few months ago, I read an online article announcing the

Press-Register—Alabama's oldest newspaper—had just printed their last edition. After more than 250 years of producing newspapers, the media outlet made the transition to digital content only. I was left feeling a bit nostalgic. I remember seeing that newspaper rolled up in a plastic bag and waiting at the end of our driveway every day during my childhood years. I remember my parents reading it. The reality that my children are growing up in a world where newspapers are no longer essential is kind of sad. However, even with fewer and fewer physical newspapers there will never be a shortage of actual news (or consumers of it) in our world. Put simply, news is a report of something that has happened, and humans are endlessly drawn to it.

In order to truly grasp the gospel of Jesus Christ, the first thing we need to understand is that it is *news*. Our word "gospel" in English is a translation of the Greek word *euangelion*, which literally means "good news" or "good message."[1] This definition immediately brings some clarity as we seek to distinguish the biblical gospel from the many false gospels we encounter. Just as a newspaper is filled with reports rather than instructions—a newspaper isn't going to explain how to work a washing machine—the gospel is not instruction about what we must do but, rather, a declaration of what has already been done. Contrary to what some believe, the gospel is not deciding to clean up your act, pray a prayer, walk a church aisle, sign a commitment card, or be baptized. No, the gospel is the proclamation of something good that has already happened. So, what happened? Why is it good? And what in the world does it have to do with identity?

In his letter to the Ephesian Church, the Apostle Paul refers to his readers as those who "heard the word of truth, the gospel of your salvation, and believed in him" (Eph. 1:13). This is the first time the word gospel is used in Ephesians, and here Paul defines it simply as "the word of truth." In a different letter, the Apostle succinctly sums up the content of this word of truth:

> *"For I delivered to you as of first importance what I also received: that Christ died for our sins in accordance with the Scriptures, that he was buried, that he was raised on the third day in accordance with the Scriptures, and that he appeared to Cephas, then to the twelve" (1 Cor. 15: 3–5).*

In summary, the gospel is the good news of Jesus Christ's life, death, and resurrection for sinners. The sad reality, however, is that many women (even professing Christians) have not truly believed this good news—this "word of truth"—because they have not grasped their own desperate need for it. Without the bad news, there is no good news. The gospel is only necessary and gloriously good when shining brightly against the dark and dirty backdrop of our ultimate human problem: sin.

We cannot receive God's salvation until we understand our need. And we cannot embrace a freely given identity in Christ until we understand and admit the ways sin has marred our truest selves. In Ephesians 1, Paul outlines the many benefits of identity in Christ—we are chosen, adopted, redeemed, and forgiven, to name but a few—but in chapter 2, he circles back to remind believers why we needed this new identity in the first place.

You (don't) have a good heart

I once asked my second grade Sunday school class how Adam and Eve sinned against God. One little boy answered, "They didn't follow directions." While it is true that God's first children failed to follow his clear directive, to sum up their sin in this way softens the blow of the offense. Failure to follow directions could sound like an honest mistake, maybe the result of absentmindedness or not listening well. In reality, Adam's and Eve's disobedience was much worse than a thoughtless error; it was abject treason against their Creator and King, leading to the fall of the human race and the corruption of the whole world.

Have you ever heard someone say, "I've made some mistakes, but that's not really who I am—deep down I have a good heart"? Most of us will readily admit we are not perfect, but we often view our own sin as a series of honest mistakes or failure to follow directions. The "gospel(s) of self" assure us that we are basically good people—people who have the power to overcome our own flaws with enough effort. Although we naturally want to believe we are virtuous, grace debunks the prevalent myth that we are born with a fundamentally good nature (Ps. 14:1–3, Jer. 17:9, Rom. 3).

In Ephesians 2:1–3, Paul declares the bad news that made the gospel necessary in the first place:

> "And you were dead in the trespasses and sins, in which you once walked, following the course of this world, following the prince of the power of the air, the spirit that is now at work in the sons of disobedience—among whom we all once lived in the passions of our flesh, carrying out the desires of the body and the mind, and were by nature children of wrath, like the rest of mankind."

Ouch!

This passage tells us that no one has a good heart. We are not, in fact, basically good people who just happen to mess up here and there; rather, we are each born with a fundamentally sinful nature that leaves no part of us uncorrupted. In other words, we aren't sinners because we sin; we sin because we are sinners. While this doesn't mean that we're as bad as we could possibly be, or even that all people are equally wicked, it does mean that all of us fall short of God's holy standard, failing to worship, obey, and glorify him as we were created to do (Rom. 3:23). It means that our desires and passions, and our feelings, minds, and bodies have all been tainted by sin.

Ephesians 2:1 tells us that all humans are born spiritually *dead*. Just as a physically dead person cannot respond to physical stimuli, spiritually dead people cannot respond to spiritual stimuli—the things of God.[2] In our dead state we are slaves to sin and rebels against God's truth. We continually disobey our Creator, following the world, the devil, and the passions of our fallen flesh rather than God's good Word. As a result, we deserve his righteous wrath.

This is a far cry from the warm, fuzzy messages of self-goodness we are saturated with by the world. The gospel is only good news when juxtaposed with the bad news of our utter depravity. "Basically good" people don't need a bloody, substitutionary Savior. While the rest of us sin because we're sinners, Jesus Christ was the only human born into this world with a truly good heart. He is the only human who perfectly obeyed the Father, and the forgiveness God offers us through him is only good news when we know just how desperately we need it.

(Don't) Believe in yourself

"She believed she could, so she did." I see this popular quote everywhere. It's printed on t-shirts, car decals, decorative signs, and posted on social media. Of course, many women have accomplished amazing things, but this message cuts God out of the picture and implies that anything is achievable with enough faith in ourselves. *Believe in yourself!* is a popular exhortation that, frankly, we love to hear. Insisting we're each wise and self-sufficient enough to chart our own course feels empowering. But while this sounds like good news, belief in self is the essence of a false gospel totally at odds with the biblical gospel of grace.

The spirit of this false gospel is epitomized in Glennon Doyle's wildly popular memoir *Untamed*. In this New York Times bestseller, Glennon recounts her journey of breaking free from the constraints of objective morality and finding "salvation" within herself. She writes:

> "If what I've found in the deep is just my self—if what I've learned is not how to commune with God but how to commune with myself—if who I have learned to trust is not God but myself—and if, for the rest of my life, no matter how lost I get, I know exactly where and how to find myself again—well, then. That is certainly enough of a miracle for me."[3]

Millions of women have consumed the content of this book, internalizing the lie that our lostness is resolved simply by finding and trusting *ourselves*. But the Bible tells us we're not self-sufficient; we're desperately needy. Not only do we require God to meet our physical needs, we also must depend on him to meet our ultimate spiritual need. Is there anyone more helpless than a dead person? Is there anyone more in need of salvation than a child of wrath? Spiritually dead people are powerless when it comes to their real problem—sin and separation from God. No amount of self-belief can resurrect a dead heart and reconcile a sinner back to God, but the gospel of grace has the power to make dead people alive *in Christ* (Eph. 2:5). Why? Because Christ is the perfect, powerful one who conquered sin and death. He's done for us what we cannot do for ourselves.

In Ephesians 2, Paul continues, "For by grace you have been saved through faith. And this is not your own doing; it is the gift of God, not a result of works, so that no one may boast" (Eph. 2:8–9). In the West, we esteem those who are accomplished and self-made through hard work. We say (or at least think) things like, "God helps those who help themselves!" This is one reason the good news of God's grace is so counterintuitive and difficult for us to receive. It can't be earned through hard work or self-made righteousness. Grace is the free gift of God's undeserved favor, which is accessed only by faith in the right person (spoiler alert, that person is not you!). Jesus Christ is the only human who lived the sinless life we have all failed to live and died the gruesome death we deserved to die, absorbing the righteous wrath of God for our sins. Jesus is the only one who can truly save us. We don't need to believe in ourselves; we need to believe in him (Acts 16:31). But what does belief entail? Is it simply agreeing with the facts that Jesus is God's Messiah, sent to earth from heaven, crucified unjustly by evil men, raised and vindicated by the Father as the perfect atonement for sinners? Belief in Jesus is not less than intellectual acceptance of these crucial facts. But it is certainly more! Even Satan and his demons understand who Jesus is (Mk. 1:23–24; Lk. 4:41). True belief involves not only acknowledgement of the facts about Jesus but also total dependence upon him.

I don't know about you, but one reason I enjoy flying on an airplane is that (once I've taken my seat) no part of reaching the destination depends on me. As the plane speeds along the runway, I don't head to the cockpit to help the pilot get the aircraft off the ground. I certainly don't begin wildly flapping my arms like a bird! No, I simply sit in my seat until we land. This action demonstrates more than just intellectual belief that the plane can fly. By coming on board and sitting down, I exhibit total reliance upon the aircraft and the pilot. I contribute nothing and trust implicitly. In the same way, to have faith in Jesus is not just to believe in your head that he saves sinners in general, but to totally depend on him to save *you*.

The gospel is not a self-esteem or self-improvement plan. On the contrary, God's grace humbles us by revealing our desperate need for a rescuer and our powerlessness to save ourselves. Grace rips the rug of self-righteousness from under our feet, bringing us low, before raising us in Christ. Jesus didn't die a bloody death on the cross to help us have faith in *ourselves*; he died so that we might place our faith in *him*. True, biblical faith means resting in Christ alone for salvation. Self-belief will eventually crush us under constant striving and ultimate failure, but belief in Christ leads us to a hope that won't disappoint (Rom. 5:2–5).

(Don't) Be true to yourself

When we were seniors in high school, my friends and I joked about spending the summer after graduation in Europe. We would quip, "Before we go to college, let's travel to Paris and

17

find ourselves!" We weren't serious, but at some point along the way we had picked up on the widely held belief that each person must discover her own identity and live in line with that truth. "Live *your* truth" is a key mantra of the gospel of self, but the gospel of grace simplifies our identity quest by enabling us to know and live *the* truth about ourselves and everything else.

Although it's hard to fathom while looking into the face of a precious newborn baby, every human being is born into this world "dead in sin" (Eph. 2:1). Paul explains how we all live true to this identity by continually disobeying God's Word and obeying our corrupted desires instead. As sinners governed by our "truth" rather than God's, we are destined for his wrath (Eph. 2:3). The gospel, however, hinges on two crucial words in Ephesians 2:4: "But God." These words are the glorious turning point in a passage that's been quite depressing thus far. Paul writes:

> "But God, being rich in mercy, because of the great love with which he loved us, even when we were dead in our trespasses, made us alive together with Christ—by grace you have been saved—and raised us up with him and seated us with him in the heavenly places in Christ Jesus, so that in the coming ages, he might show the immeasurable riches of his grace in kindness toward us in Christ Jesus" (Eph. 2:4–7).

The good news of grace is not only that God saves sinners from his wrath, but also that he makes spiritually dead people alive by uniting them to his Son. In Christ, we receive a brand-new nature and identity, leading to new desires (Eph. 2:5–6). Grace beckons us to come to Christ just as we are, but it never leaves us that way. The gospel makes us new! Coupled with Christ's call to believe the gospel is a call to repent (Mk. 1:15). Repentance is a change of heart and mind that leads to a change of direction. Jesus said, "If anyone would come after me, let him deny himself and take up his cross and follow me" (Mk. 8:34). Far from a call to be true to ourselves, Jesus commands us to deny the passions and desires of the sinful identity that once defined us and live true to our new identity in him.

Of this passage, pastor and author Sam Allberry writes, "It is the same for us all… I am to deny myself, take up my cross and follow him… Denying yourself does not mean tweaking your behavior here and there. It is saying 'no' to your deepest sense of who you are, for the sake of Christ…" He continues, "the fact is that the gospel demands everything of all of us. If someone thinks the gospel has somehow slotted into their life quite easily, without causing any major adjustments to their lifestyle or aspirations, it is just as likely that they have not started following Jesus at all."[4]

Jesus doesn't make good people better; he makes dead people alive. The gospel renders us new creations in Christ. By faith, we share with Jesus in his death as our old self is crucified, and we share with him in his resurrection as we are raised to a brand-new nature in him (2 Cor. 5:17). In Christ, we receive the Holy Spirit, who enables us to put off the deeds characteristic of our former identity and put on Christ-like living that matches our new identity (Rom. 8:13; Eph. 4:22). Grace frees us to stop trying to be true to our sinful selves and, instead, devote our lives to good works that are true to Christ (Eph. 2:10).

Summing it up

As I sat face-to-face with the confused fifteen-year-old girl in the counseling office that day, my heart broke for her. What should I tell her? Well, I could have heralded the gospel of moralism, suggesting she get her act together and promising that God accepts those whose good deeds outweigh their bad. I could have offered her the prosperity gospel, exhorting her to "have more faith" so God would bless her school career and social life. I could have leaned into the therapeutic gospel, telling her that God exists to meet her felt needs and make her happy. Or perhaps it wouldn't even matter what I told her as the pluralistic gospel says, "all roads lead to God" as long as one's religious beliefs are held with sincerity. But of course, I didn't offer her any of these false gospels—these shams for the real thing. I gave her the "word of truth" instead. Only the biblical gospel of grace tells us, "We are more sinful and flawed in ourselves than we ever dared believe, yet at the very same time we are more loved and accepted in Jesus Christ than we ever dared hope."[5] Many women have been in church for years and haven't believed this gospel. Have you believed it? It is truly our only hope.

Questions for reflection and discussion

1. What does the word "gospel" literally mean? Explain the difference between news and instruction. How does this help us distinguish the biblical gospel from false gospels?

2. If you were explaining the gospel to the fifteen-year-old sitting in my office, what would you say?

3. Read Ephesians 2:1–3. What's wrong with the statement "She made a mistake, but that's not really who she is; deep down she has a good heart"?

4. Read Ephesians 2:8–9. Why is the exhortation to "believe in yourself" at odds with the gospel of grace? Why can't belief in self save us?

5. When it comes to belief in Jesus (biblical faith), what is the difference between intellectual assent and dependent trust? (Hint: Remember the airplane illustration!) Explain why both are important.

6. Read Ephesians 2:4–6, 10. What change in our identity does God's grace bring? How does this enable us to be true to Christ rather than to ourselves?

7. Have you believed the gospel of grace, repented of your sins, and put your faith in Christ alone for salvation? If not, what's stopping you from doing so today?

2

Every Spiritual Blessing

Benefits of gospel identity

Blessed be the God and Father of our Lord Jesus Christ,
who has blessed us in Christ with every spiritual blessing
in the heavenly places.
—Ephesians 1:3

I spent the summer after my freshman year of college working as a counselor at a summer camp for girls. To help us get to know one another before campers arrived, each counselor was asked to write a piece entitled "I Am From" to share with the other counselors and staff. We were supposed to detail the various people, places, things, and experiences that had helped shape us. Here are just a few things I wrote down about my (fairly naive) first eighteen years of life:

> "I am from small-town Alabama where everyone knows your name. I am from my dad's passion for truth and my mom's servant-hearted love. I am from long runs, good books, and deep quotes. I am from true friendships and

*necessary break-ups, from Monday night family Bible study
and countless study sessions for school. I am from striving,
the stress of perfectionism, and lots of good grades that
won't matter in the end."*

Although I wrote the piece years ago, I still remember enjoying
the introspection it required. Reflecting on where I was from
(both literally and figuratively) revealed and explained something
about the young woman I had become. It explained some of the
things that made me uniquely *me*. My enjoyment of this activity
likely has something to do with how I've always loved a good
writing project, but it also hints at the human desire to know
who we truly are—that human longing for a sense of identity.

Human beings, particularly in the West, are obsessed with
self-discovery. We see this in the wide-spread popularity of
personality tests like the Myers-Briggs Type Indicator and, more
recently, the Enneagram. We see it in the hundreds of "Which
___ are you?" quizzes on social media sites: "Which cake are
you? Are you a classic chocolate, a spicy carrot, or an adorable
cupcake? Take our quiz to find out."[1] The desire for self-discovery
sucks us in, and before long we've not only identified with a type
of cake but we've also determined which sandwich, breed of
dog, and Disney Princess we are!

As we saw in the previous chapter, our culture tells us we each
have an authentic identity that needs to be uncovered, not so
much by internet quizzes, but by looking deep within. In order
to flourish, the world says not only must we discover and define
who we are, we must also be true to ourselves. We saw that
the gospel simplifies our search by granting us a new identity
in Christ. Unfortunately, though, our gospel identity doesn't

always seem to make inroads into the way we actually perceive ourselves. While many of us have been taught to find who we are in Christ, this can seem like a trite, theological simplification of our unique personhood that doesn't always scratch the itch for greater self-discovery and validation. This is because our quest to find ourselves is driven by two bigger questions that plague us as women: *Do I possess true worth?* and *What are the sources and measures of my worth?* These are the concerns driving our need to know and prove that we are wanted, loved, and secure. In order to become truly gospel-shaped women, we desperately need to understand how our identity in Christ comes to bear on these particular questions.

For the love of categories

There are many features that make a particular woman unique—personality, physical appearance, talents, preferences, and proclivities, just to name a few. In addition, numerous factors influence a particular woman's life—her ethnicity, culture, family history, socioeconomic status, religious upbringing, relationships, roles, work, life experiences, and sufferings. All these categories shape a woman's sense of personal identity, helping her understand herself and her place in the world.[2]

As young children, our sense of self is very much tied to the category of family. We first understand ourselves in relation to those with whom we belong. My second son clearly demonstrated this fact a few years ago when another little boy asked him, "Who are you?" Without even pausing to think, my son replied, "I'm one of my dad's boys." At five years old, his entire sense of self was (quite adorably) bound up in being a son and a brother... so much so that he didn't even share his own name. As we grow in age and independence, we begin to look to categories outside of family to gain a sense of self. We look to our experiences, our physical appearance, our preferences and attractions, the work or hobbies we excel at, and the relationships we have beyond our family. We often use categories to tell others about ourselves and to describe how we spend our days.

For example, the bio on my Instagram profile reads: "Sarah Rice—pastor's wife, boy mom x4, writer, and biblical counselor." This bio reveals some things about me through categories. It tells you about my primary relationships and roles: I'm a wife and a mother of four boys. It tells you about my work and God-given gifts: I care for children, counsel, and write articles and books. If you go beyond the biographical information and look at the photos and captions I post, you'll learn more about me through categories. You'll see what I look like. You'll read about the things I do, the things I love, and the things I struggle with. You may even learn something about my background through the pictures I share and the stories I tell.

These categories are not random or insignificant; they are ordained by a sovereign God, and they affect and shape us as individual women. We run into problems, however, when we rely on categories to do more than just describe the particulars of our own lives and instead look to them to define us as people—to tell us who we are and why we matter. In our quest for self-discovery, we often look to one or more of our categories to be the source of our identity and measure of our worth, and this is ultimately crushing.

For instance, if I look to the category of motherhood as my primary source of identity, and if I believe that my worth as a woman rises and falls based on how well I perform in this role, what happens when my children leave the nest? Or when they greatly disappoint me? Or when I'm faced with my own many failures as a mother? In all these cases, I will feel despair and the loss of my sense of self. What if work and a successful career are the primary sources of your identity and sense of worth? What happens when you don't perform well at your job or when someone criticizes your work? What if you lose your job or are unable to work because of chronic health problems or other unforeseen circumstances? Your sense of self-worth will plummet. What if our identity as women is rooted in having the love of a significant other, a beautiful face, a certain sized body, or a comfortably large bank balance? When the waves of age, change, loss, unfulfilled desires, and unmet expectations crash into us, we sink.

While categories can describe how we are and what we do, no category can ultimately tell us who we are. Categories may affect and shape our *sense* of identity, but they are not the *source* of our identity. In other words, the categories into which you and I fall can *describe* us but they cannot *ascribe* us worth. We were not made to "find ourselves" in any category, be it family, career, marriage, parenting, finances, health, physical appearance, or friendships. These features and factors constantly fluctuate and are fleeting. These are very thin wires on which to hang the heavy questions we each wrestle with when it comes to our sense of worth: Am I wanted? Am I loved? Am I good enough? Am I secure? While much of what we experience in this life has the ability to shape us, only one thing (one person, rather) has the power to define us.

Created woman in God's image

The first thing the Bible tells us about God is that he is the Creator; therefore, the first thing the Bible tells us about ourselves is that we are created beings (Gen. 1). This truth—that human beings did not self-originate—has huge implications for our identity. Because God is the author of our existence, we belong to him and our identity is inextricably tied to him. Our Creator alone can define us and tell us who we truly are.

The Bible teaches that human beings are the only part of God's creation made in his very own image. Genesis 1:27 says, "So God created man in his own image, in the image of God he created him; male and female he created them." What is it to be made in the image of God, and what does this mean for our identity as women?

Humans uniquely reflect God in ways other parts of the created order do not. For example, human beings, unlike plants and animals, are moral creatures with the capacity for language, reasoning, creativity, committed relationships, and the exercise of authority. More recently scholars have pointed out that the phrase "image of God" denotes a royal representative. In ancient Eastern societies, the king alone was "the image of god." As the sole human believed to have access to the god(s), he visibly represented and ruled on behalf of the unseen deity. He was the mediator between the people and the gods.[3]

When you put all of this together, the Bible's claim that all humans are made in the image of God is quite incredible. The Almighty God of the universe, who is an invisible Spirit, created every single human being to be a visual representation of him. We were made to live in relationship with God, reflecting the goodness and glory of his nature to the world. We were called to mediate between the Creator and the rest of his creation by taking dominion of the created order and lovingly ruling on his behalf (Gen. 1:28). And we were made to do this as distinctly gendered beings.

God created men and women to bear his image. Both men and women (together and as individuals) reflect the truth about God more clearly than any other part of the created order. The very core of my identity and yours is being a woman made in the image of God, and the woman part is not some insignificant footnote; it is the very expression of our personhood.[4] You and I image God in our womanhood. This has less to do with our own sense of gender, our roles in any particular season, or our embodiment of cultural stereotypes of femininity; it has everything to do with the gender our good God assigned to us in our biology and called "very good" (Gen. 1:31).

We are made to image the inestimable worth of the God of the universe *as women*, and this is the very source of our unchangeable identity, dignity, and worth. Yet, if this is true, why do we constantly feel the need to discover our own unique identity and prove our own worth? And why is it that, deep down, we feel so unworthy?

Identity crisis

When he was fifty, my father-in-law shocked all his kids by buying a Porsche. I'm not sure if this fast, fancy sports car was part of a mid-life crisis, but it certainly seemed uncharacteristic for an outdoorsman who always drove a truck and loved hunting and fishing in the country. (It was a fun car that we all enjoyed, nonetheless!) We've all heard of the mid-life identity crisis. As people age and change, they sometimes engage in unusual (and, at times, ridiculous) behaviors because of a perceived loss of their sense of self. In a much more catastrophic way, the entrance of sin into the world led to a major human identity crisis.

When the first image-bearers saw that the fruit of the one tree God had declared off-limits was desirable, they fell prey to the destructive lie that being a creature of the Creator was undesirable. As our first parents doubted God's goodness and questioned his love, suddenly being accountable to their Maker felt like oppression, rather than true freedom. When they plucked the fruit, they grasped for independence. As they sank their teeth into what God had forbidden, they foolishly clenched self-determination—the right to define their own morality, create their own identity, and chart their own course. But instead of finding freedom and joy, Adam and Eve found themselves enslaved to corruption, separated from the God of all life, and filled with shame.

Like a once-flawless statue violently desecrated, the image of God in humanity was horrifically marred by sin. Although God mercifully allowed Adam and Eve to bring more image-bearers into the world, our first parents passed an inheritance of corruption to their offspring. As we saw in Ephesians 2, all human beings come into this world spiritually dead in sin and estranged from the good God we were created to reflect.

In our sin, we suppress the obvious truth God has embedded in the created order and resist his rightful claim on our lives (Rom. 1:18–21). Blinded to his goodness and glory, we hotly pursue self-rule and ascribe to ourselves a self-made worth—worth disconnected from our truly worthy Creator. This is idolatry, and it keeps us from rightly perceiving our true identity and value. The Bible says that our self-perceived wisdom makes us fools who devalue ourselves and other people (Rom. 1:26–32).

This is why there is so much confusion, heartache, and flat-out rebellion when it comes to issues of bodily autonomy, the sacredness of every human life, the goodness of gender distinction, and God's design for our bodies and sexuality. It's why we're all on a never-ending mission to discover our unique selves and prove our worthiness through categories like work, roles, relationships, and physical appearance. And it's why we always seem to come up short on this quest. These various issues are not disconnected; they're all symptoms of the human identity crisis that resulted from the fall.

The world tells us that when the reality of our personal identity crisis presses in, we must look deeper into ourselves to resolve the crisis: *Believe in yourself! You're a good person! You're strong! You're enough!* As encouraging as these words may sound, they ring hollow—we simply can't fix this crisis of our own making. As we saw in the previous chapter, faith in self can't assuage the shame and guilt that weigh heavy on us, and no amount of positive self-talk can totally free us from the need we feel to prove our worth. No portion of self-love can erase the deep-down nagging thought: *Maybe I'm not really lovable.*

The reason is this: Although we have unshakeable worth and value as women made in the image of God—regardless of whether we're a Christian or not—apart from him we are *not* worthy. Left to ourselves, we are not good, and we are not enough. We've done nothing to merit God's favor or love; in fact, we've merited his wrath (Rom. 3:23). To truly appreciate the God-given value all people possess as image-bearers, and to be made truly righteous, we somehow need to be reunited to God himself. This is why the gospel is such good news and why our identity in Christ has such powerful and life-changing benefits.

The gospel identity: Union with Christ

Following the opening greeting of his letter to the Ephesians, Paul bursts out in praise to God: "Blessed be the God and Father of our Lord Jesus Christ, who has blessed us in Christ with every spiritual blessing in the heavenly places" (Eph. 1:3). Paul praises God the Father for the many spiritual benefits he has bestowed on those who are true believers. Because we tend to long for tangible, earthly blessings—a successful career, a fulfilling marriage, healthy children, material comforts—spiritual blessings can sound a bit abstract or even boring. The truth, however, is that earthly blessings are temporary and ultimately futile apart from spiritual blessedness. Commentator Matthew Henry says it well: "spiritual and heavenly blessings [are] the best blessings, with which we cannot be miserable and without which we cannot be but so."[5]

Before looking at these spiritual blessings, we need to focus on a tiny but crucial phrase in Paul's opening doxology—*in Christ*. Paul uses this phrase (or some equivalent such as *in him*) 164 times in all his writings and ten times in Ephesians 1 alone.[6] Clearly, this is not a meaningless expression to gloss over but one with huge implications!

When Paul writes "in Christ" he is referring to the believer's new identity as one who is united to Jesus. In other words, when a sinner hears the good news of the gospel and believes, she is not only saved from God's wrath but also inseparably united to Jesus and brought back into fellowship with God the Father through him. Because this glorious reality is difficult to wrap our minds around, the Bible uses a number of metaphors to help us: We're like branches connected to Jesus the vine (Jn. 15:1–7), we're united to Jesus like a wife to her husband (Eph. 5:22–33), Jesus is the head and we are parts of his body (1 Cor. 12:12–27), and we are a temple built of many stones with Christ as the chief cornerstone (Eph. 2:20–22). Each word picture helps us grasp what theologians refer to as "union with Christ."[7]

New Testament Professor Timothy G. Gombis says it this way:

> "The people of God are not merely loved by God or saved by God; we are brought back into God. God has done something outrageous to us, bringing us into Christ so that we now have a completely new location on the cosmic map... We are now 'in Christ,' which becomes our fundamental identity, opening up for us an entirely new range of options for behavior, relationships, patterns of thought, and speech, and the future trajectory of our lives. We are caught up into the love relationship that God shares between God the Father and Jesus Christ, his Son."[8]

To be in Christ means that Jesus is our representative before God, so that everything true about him becomes true about us. Namely, Christ's sinless life and perfect obedience to the Father are counted as ours, and his atoning death on the cross has paid our immense sin debt in full. Incredibly, Christ's righteousness is credited to us, so that when God looks at believers, he sees the perfection of his Son rather than image-bearers marred by sin. In Christ, our position is worthiness before God, and his heart is full of affection toward us!

To be *in Christ* also means that Christ is *in us* through the Holy Spirit, who dwells within every believer. The Spirit makes believers spiritually alive by giving us a brand-new nature and helping us increasingly live into it by turning away from sin and growing in obedience. This means we're not only worthy before God in our position, but we're also gradually becoming worthy in our practice. This process is slow and sometimes one step forward and two steps back. And when progress feels slow, it is so important to remember our position in Christ. This position gives us confidence to draw near to God and receive his help in our struggle against remaining sin (Heb. 4:16).

Benefits of gospel identity (Union with Christ)

Can you imagine having something so real and permanent that not even death itself could take it from you? Can you fathom being given an identity in someone else that makes you more—not less—of who you really are? Can you conceive of possessing incredible worth that isn't dependent on your performance or accomplishments? Can you comprehend being stunningly beautiful in a way that will only increase rather than diminish as you age and mature? This is what we have in our union with Christ! Our identity *in Christ* enables us to abandon the desperate search to find our true selves because we've been found by God in his Son. Our union with Christ gives us eternal rest from striving to be enough because he is enough for us, and he is remaking us into his likeness. Ephesians 1:3–11 goes on to outline some of the many spiritual blessings we possess in Christ. It's these blessings that give us deep assurance and hope when the internal questions about our own worth plague us.

Chosen

> *"He chose us in him before the foundation of the world, that we should be holy and blameless before him" (Eph. 1:4).*

If you are in Christ, you no longer need to wonder if you are deeply wanted. Before the foundations of the world were laid, God set his sights on *you* and chose *you* to be his own. The text says he chose you for a purpose—to make you holy and blameless. Before you were born and had done anything bad or good, God determined that, through Jesus, he would renew his own perfect image in you. Jesus Christ—both truly God and truly man—is said to be the image of the invisible God (Col. 1:15), the exact imprint of God's perfect nature (Heb.1:3). Christ is both the ultimate picture of God and the ultimate picture of what humans should be, and God is conforming his chosen ones into the spotless image of his Son (Rom. 8:29).

Loved

> *"In love he predestined us for adoption to himself as sons through Jesus Christ, according to the purpose of his will, to the praise of his glorious grace, with which he has blessed us in the Beloved" (Eph. 1:4–6).*

If you are in Christ, you can cease striving to prove to yourself and others that you are worthy of love. This passage says it was because of love that God predetermined to make you part of his forever family—the church. Although sin spiritually orphaned you, God adopted you as his own, giving you all the love, rights, and privileges of a true daughter through his faithful Son. God did this, not because he foresaw something good or lovable in you, but simply because it was his purpose and perfect will to do so. Because God is love, it pleased him to bless you in Christ. In spite of your sin, you are deeply known, deeply loved, and fully accepted into the family of God.

Forgiven

> "In him we have redemption through his blood, the forgiveness of our trespasses, according to the riches of his grace" (Eph. 1:7).

If you are in Christ, you can reject the belief that true freedom comes through independence from God—through rejecting and escaping his rules. You can also lay down the heavy burden of trying to keep God's law perfectly in your own strength. It's your own sinful nature, not God's law, that enslaves you. You cannot eradicate the deep roots of your heart's corruption by rule-keeping. Neither breaking the rules in rebellion, nor endlessly striving to obey them in your own power, will assuage the guilt and shame you feel deep inside. You must face the truth: On your own, you are not good enough, but through union with Jesus, you are redeemed and fully forgiven. In Christ, God set you free from slavery to sin, self, and Satan. Christ's bloody atonement paid your debt in full and wiped your slate clean. Your guilt is removed, and your shame is covered.

Secure

> *"In him we have obtained an inheritance, having been predestined according to the purpose of him who works all things according to the counsel of his will" (Eph. 1:11).*

If you are in Christ, you don't need to seek security in temporal things like material wealth, career success, and good health. God has adopted you as his daughter, therefore you are his *heir*—a fellow heir with Christ (Rom. 8:17). In Christ, you have obtained an inheritance that won't perish or fade (1 Pet. 1:4). This means everything Christ inherits as the ultimate Son of God, you will also inherit, and this inheritance can never be diminished or lost. You are eternally secure!

You may be wondering, "Well, what *is* this inheritance?" First and foremost, your inheritance is God himself. Because of sin, you were once "without God in the world" (Eph. 2:12), but, in Christ, you've been brought into an intimate relationship with your Maker (Eph. 2:13, 18). You get God's very presence for all eternity (Rev. 21:3)! Second, your inheritance is the world and everything in it. Ephesians 1:10 tells us God is uniting *all* things in Christ—"things in heaven and things on earth." Jesus is making all things new, and one day he will visibly reign over a perfectly restored earth. In Christ, you will inherit this new world and all the good things in it. Third, your inheritance will include a glorified physical body—a body that will no longer struggle with sin, sickness, and identity issues (Rom. 8:23). This new body will fully enjoy God and his gifts rightly.[9] Why in the world would God grant sinners like us such a magnificent inheritance (in addition to every other spiritual blessing)? Ephesians 1:12 tells us: "so that we who were the first to hope in Christ might be to the praise of his glory."

Summing it up

Remember the "I Am From" piece I was asked to write so many years ago? I concluded it with these words:

> *"I am from years of seeking to find my worth in myself apart from Christ, but I am also from years of God's grace. He has slowly but surely moved in my heart, helping me understand that only an intimate relationship with him through Jesus will ever truly define and fulfill me. I am from the Lord and from his love, and nothing can take that away."*

Only the love of God in Christ can tell you who you really are and transform you into who you were created to be. Only the gospel has the power to save and shape your soul for abundant life on earth and eternity in the presence of God. Because it's only when the love of Christ takes hold of you—when Christ dwells in your heart through faith—that you're filled up with the fullness of God (Eph. 3:19), a fullness that overflows into every sphere of your life. This is gospel-shaped womanhood. This is my prayer for me and you.

Questions for reflection and discussion

1. What categories do you primarily use to describe yourself and to tell others how you spend your days?

2. Which category are you most tempted to look to as a source of your identity and as a measure of your worth? How have you been let down when you try to do this? Explain.

3. Read Genesis 1:27–28. What does it mean to be made in the image of God and what implications does this have for our identity?

4. How has sin marred the image of God in humanity, leading us all into an identity crisis?

5. What is the difference between possessing worth and being worthy?

6. The gospel is not only good news for our eternal salvation but also for our identity now. Read Ephesians 1:3. What does it mean to be in Christ? What does it mean that Christ is in us?

7. Based on Ephesians 1:3–12, how does being in Christ bring lasting assurance that we are deeply wanted, loved, forgiven, and secure?

8. Are you resting in your identity and worth in Christ day by day? Ask the Lord to help you turn away from seeking to find your primary identity in anything but him.

3

True Female Empowerment

The indwelling Holy Spirit

In him, you also, when you heard the word of truth,
the gospel of your salvation, and believed in him,
were sealed with the promised Holy Spirit, who is
the guarantee of our inheritance until we acquire
possession of it, to the praise of his glory.
—Ephesians 1:13–14

It was Super Bowl Sunday night in February 2020, and we were gathered in the living room for the football game. Truth be told, I was there for the family time rather than the football. I folded laundry, tended to our baby, and paid little attention to the TV until the loud music and glitzy-costumed superstars of the halftime show piqued my interest. Two successful, attractive, physically fit female singers, aged fifty and forty-three, commanded the attention of millions from the stage. While their performance turned many heads, it also raised a few eyebrows. Their costumes were as skimpy as they were flashy, and—for all the talent they possessed—their hip-thrusting, pole-dancing routines were provocative, to say the least. As the show progressed, my husband and I became increasingly uncomfortable with what we and our young sons were witnessing. We turned off the television until the football game resumed.

In the days following the Super Bowl, the internet buzzed with commentary about the halftime performance. Some said the immodest costumes and explicit choreography devalued these women by presenting them as sexual objects, even if it was freely chosen. Others said the show empowered women everywhere by showcasing the autonomy of these female superstars through their talent, beauty, sexuality, and influence. The whole conversation got me thinking deeply about the hot topic of female empowerment.

What is female empowerment anyway?

While the phrase brings a host of issues to mind, "female empowerment" (in a general sense) means raising the status of women by equipping them with *more:* more rights, more freedom, more education, more opportunities, more resources, and more control over their lives. This broad synopsis begs a fundamental question: Why does the status of women need to be raised in the first place? It's no secret that throughout history, and even today, many cultures and peoples have denigrated and oppressed women, failing to rightly esteem them as image-bearers of God. The comparative weakness of the female body to the male body has led many to view women as inferior, and, sadly, many women have faced domination and abuse at the hands of their male counterparts. In her book *The Secular Creed*, Rebecca McLaughlin notes that, in ancient cultures, the relative physical weakness of women was understood by men as a license for domination: "In Greco-Roman thinking, men were superior to women, and sex was a way to prove it... The idea that every woman had the right to choose what happened to her own body would've been laughable."[1] Sadly, in this fallen world many men still use women as objects for their own purposes and pleasure.

Even in a modern, Western nation like the United States of America—a nation founded on the belief that all humans are created equal and possess certain natural rights—women were historically denied some of the opportunities and liberties afforded to men. American women in the early 1800s were not widely educated and had few opportunities to make a living outside the home; they were also denied the right to vote in most cases and were often unable to own property. Even after ratification of the 19th Amendment in 1920 (which granted American women the right to vote), many women of color were still disenfranchised and denied other basic rights.

As an American woman, raised in an upper-middle class home almost two centuries later, I experienced a different reality. My family, school, and community highly valued education and opportunities for women. I enrolled in honors courses in high school, took college entrance exams, and spent years preparing for higher education. I swam in cultural waters that said a woman could do whatever she wanted to do—anything a man could do and more. It was the age of "girl power" when the world told women we could have it all: the fulfilling career, the lovely family, and even control over men through beauty and sexual prowess. Today, the world shouts to my children's generation that, not only can a woman *do* anything a man does, but she can also *be* a man if she so desires. It seems that "female empowerment" now even includes the (supposed) freedom to break through the boundaries of biological sex and choose a different gender. But how can we claim women's rights are necessary and important if womanhood itself is fluid?

Clearly, there is cultural confusion about what female empowerment entails. Are women empowered by education and equal rights? Are we empowered by the belief that there really are no gender distinctions, so we can be and do anything we want? Are we empowered by a "no rules" sexual freedom that isn't suppressed by taboos or the patriarchy? On one hand, the world says our bodies are irrelevant and we're more than what we can offer a man sexually; yet, the functional message to women through every media outlet is, "You sure better have a good body and sex appeal!" The world is confused about female empowerment because it doesn't know a woman's true source of power. In fact, the world rejects the only real foundation we have for women's rights.

The real basis for women's rights

The *imago Dei* (Latin for "image of God") is the only foundation for the inherent dignity and value of every single human person, regardless of age, gender, race, ability, or any other factor. As we saw in the previous chapter, humans are distinguished from all other animals in that they are image-bearers of the Creator (Gen. 1:27). The *imago Dei* means that male and female possess equal dignity, value, intellect, and importance. Although men and women are different in obvious and necessary ways, neither is superior or inferior to the other. The equality of men and women isn't a feminist idea; it's a biblical truth. Even so, it is easy to see how, throughout human history, image-bearers have often acted more like animals than the God they were made to reflect.

In numerous societies, the physically stronger have dominated and oppressed the weaker and more vulnerable. Because many societies down through the centuries have lacked a deep conviction regarding the *imago Dei*, they have lacked objective grounding for human rights.

Humanity's fall into sin explains the conflict between the sexes. After Adam and Eve disobeyed God, he announced how the curse of sin would radically affect their relationship, specifically within marriage. Rather than marriage being beautiful complementarity—a God-like portrayal of unity within diversity—it would now be an on-going power struggle. Wives resist the God-ordained headship of their husbands (given for their good), and husbands rule over their wives in harsh, domineering ways instead of selflessly loving and leading (Gen. 3:16). In a broader sense, men in general are now inclined to employ their God-given strength to use and abuse women rather than to honor and protect them. Because of sin, women often fear men, seeking to self-protect and rule over them through godless, loveless manipulation. What a heartbreaking departure from God's purpose for his children!

This is yet another reason why the gospel is such good news. When God the Son took on flesh as the image of the invisible God (Col. 1:15), he perfectly embodied and lived out God's intentions for his human creatures. He did this, in part, through his treatment of women:

> *"If we could read the gospels through first-century eyes, Jesus's treatment of women would knock us to our knees... Whether little girls or prostitutes, whether despised foreigners or women made unclean by menstrual blood,*

> *whether married or single, sick (Matt. 8:14–16) or disabled*
> *(Luke 13:10–16), Jesus made time for women and treated*
> *them with care and respect."*[2]

Jesus affirmed the dignity and value of women by drawing near them in love, never using or abusing them. He honored women perfectly as he extended both truth and grace to them—never ignoring or excusing sin yet offering full forgiveness and healing in him (Jn. 4:1–30; Jn. 8:1–11).

While Jesus clearly affirmed women, the Apostle Paul's writings are sometimes considered sexist at first blush. Digging into the New Testament letters, however, reveals that Paul's view of women was not contrary to Christ's. Christianity radically elevated the status of women in the ancient world through its teaching that union with Christ equalizes men and women of all classes and ethnic groups. Paul wrote, "There is neither Jew nor Greek, there is neither slave nor free, there is no male and female, for you are all one in Christ Jesus" (Gal. 3:28). In addition, Paul commanded women to learn (1 Tim. 2:11), a shocking exhortation in a culture where education was primarily for the men. He taught husbands to love their wives sacrificially as Christ loved the church (Eph. 5:25–26). Meanwhile, the Apostle Peter exhorted husbands to live with their physically weaker wives in an understanding way, honoring them as "heirs with you of the grace of life" (1 Pet. 3:7). Considering this, is it surprising that women flocked to Christianity in droves during the first century? The early church was two-thirds female and is still disproportionately female today.[3]

Rebekah Merkle reminds us to give credit where credit is due when she writes:

"The feminists try to take credit for something that is the fruit of the gospel, working its way into culture like yeast through a loaf. We need to stop letting the feminists act as if they somehow achieved our equality. Unconverted societies never treat women well, and that is extraordinarily easy to document. Women being treated with respect is fruit that grows on one kind of tree, and that tree is a cross."[4]

Power divorced from God is no power at all

In seeking to understand what empowers women, let's remember that any "power" divorced from truth, morality, and the all-powerful Creator is no real power at all. It's a lie. It follows that any cultural movement seeking to empower women apart from God and by means contrary to his Word will veer off course, responding to one sin problem (in this case, female oppression) with more sin. This is what has happened in much of the feminist movement.

First wave feminism certainly won some important rights for women, such as the ability to vote, own property, and pursue greater educational opportunities. I am so grateful to hold these rights as an American woman today. However, it's important to recognize that some of the feminist movement's most influential leaders (such as Elizabeth Cady Stanton, Susan B. Anthony, Margaret Sanger, Betty Friedan, and Gloria Steinem) were women whose worldview was completely antithetical to the Christian gospel. Some leaders went far beyond the pursuit of legal and economic equality for women as image-bearers of God. They fought for (supposed) "rights" that are fundamentally at odds with God's character, moral law, and good purposes for humanity revealed in Scripture. Among other things, second wave feminists' "equality for women" often meant a rejection of distinct gender roles. Many feminists believed women needed to be liberated from sexual oppression by pursuing a "free love" unbound by biblical sexual ethics or traditional mores. They fought for the right to abort babies in the womb—taking the lives of fellow image-bearers—because they believed this was necessary for women to possess true autonomy and equality with men.

While feminists and Christians agree women are valuable, whole persons—equal to men in dignity and worth—we are opposed when it comes to our beliefs about the source and purpose of true female empowerment. Largely, feminism is a movement of *women* seeking to empower *women* for the sake of fulfilling and glorifying *women*. And, frankly, the angry-activist, "I am woman, hear me roar!" spirit of many parts of the movement has made a confusing and ugly mess of true womanhood. Christianity, on the other hand, is a movement of *God* by which his Spirit empowers women to know their true identity and fulfill a mission that's bigger and more glorious than themselves. Far from being accomplished at the expense of women, this God-glorifying mission produces the ultimate good for women, men, and the entire cosmos.

The indwelling Holy Spirit

As women in Christ, we have an incredible source of eternal power. The Holy Spirit of God now dwells within us! In Ephesians 1:13–14, Paul writes:

> *"In him, you also when you heard the word of truth, the gospel of your salvation, and believed in him, were sealed*

with the promised Holy Spirit, who is the guarantee of our inheritance until we acquire possession of it."

Paul refers to the Spirit as "the promised Holy Spirit" because he was pledged beforehand by Christ. Before his crucifixion, Jesus promised his first disciples that the Father would send another Helper to dwell in them forever (Jn. 14:16–17). This Helper would guide them into all truth (Jn. 16:13). Later, before he ascended into heaven, Jesus said the Holy Spirit would come and empower his disciples to take the gospel to every corner of the world (Acts 1:8). The Scriptures also teach that anyone who does not have the Holy Spirit does not actually belong to Christ (Rom. 8:9). Therefore, to be a Christian woman is to be filled with the Spirit. Every Christian woman can be confident the Spirit of God miraculously brought her heart from spiritual death to life (Jn. 3:5–8) and now dwells within—sealing, empowering, and transforming her.

How does the seal of the Spirit empower us as women? Well, a seal has several purposes. First, it confirms something as genuine and true. Think of a notary embossing an official document to prove its legitimacy. The presence of the Spirit in us authenticates our true identity *in Christ*, verifying that we are "the real deal." The seal of the Spirit is proof that Christianity isn't just some "pie in the sky" theoretical game. It's all true, and we have experienced it in a personally transformative way. "The Spirit himself bears witness with our Spirit that we are children of God, and if children, then heirs" (Rom. 8:16–17).

In addition to confirming something as genuine, a seal also marks one's property. Imagine writing your son's name on the tag of his jacket to label it as belonging to him. The indwelling

Spirit labels believers as those who truly belong to God, so that we actually receive the spiritual benefits of being a true child of the Father. The Spirit applies the benefits of redemption to believers in a saving way, making general truths powerful, personal realities.

Finally, a seal functions as a stamp of security and preservation. Picture a sealed envelope keeping the contents within secure until they reach their destination. In a similar way, the Holy Spirit holds believers fast until the end when Christ returns. He is our security guard, ensuring the safety of our inheritance until we acquire full possession of it. He is like earnest money—a pledge that our eternal inheritance will one day come in fullness and never be lost or taken.[5]

True knowledge is power

Paul closes out Ephesians 1 with a prayer for the believers in Ephesus:

> "I do not cease to give thanks for you, remembering you in my prayers, that the God of our Lord Jesus Christ, the Father of Glory, may give you the Spirit of wisdom and of revelation in the knowledge of him, having the eyes of your hearts enlightened, that you may know what is the hope to which he has called you, what are the riches of his glorious inheritance in the saints, and what is the immeasurable greatness of his power toward us who believe" (Eph. 1:16–19).

You've likely heard the saying "knowledge is power." It's true because there's no real power apart from knowledge of God and his truth. Jesus claimed to be God's truth (Jn. 14:6), and he promised his disciples that abiding in his Word and knowing the Truth (him!) would set them free (Jn. 8:31–32). By and large, feminism equates female empowerment with autonomy—a woman's freedom to submit only to herself. Jesus, however, says real freedom comes only by knowing him and abiding in his Word through continual trust and obedience.

Regardless of the victories won for women's rights, women who do not know God in Christ are not truly free; they remain slaves to sin (Jn. 8:34). But the Holy Spirit breaks the bonds of sin when he makes the spiritually dead alive, revealing to believers what's true about God and themselves. He then grants them the power to act on this knowledge in obedience! Paul prays the Spirit will make believers wise by continually showing them the hope to which they've been called, the riches of their inheritance, and the great power they possess for holy living.

Hope of a world made new

Far too many women have faced brutal injustices, abuse, and oppression in this broken world we inhabit. Indeed, things are not as they should be. But our hope is not in broken women running a broken world; it's in Christ ruling a world made new! Those in Christ know the ultimate plan for the entire cosmos—God will "unite all things in him [Christ], things in heaven and things on earth" (Eph. 1:10). At the consummation of world history, Jesus will return to earth and bring cosmic reconciliation, making all things right and new (Col. 1:20). At that time, he will raise the dead from their graves and gather together all who belong to him in heaven and on earth. He will judge and eradicate evil, setting the world right by establishing one harmonious kingdom against which the gates of hell cannot prevail. In this new kingdom, men and women will live and reign together as brothers and sisters in perfect harmony and love.[6]

Worldly female empowerment is not the hope to which we've been called because women cannot ultimately right all that is wrong. Women cannot remedy the human condition or redeem the cosmos. We cannot heal all the wounds of abuse and set every captive free. Female empowerment cannot bring perfect justice for the sins committed against women or for the sins women have committed against others. But Jesus can... and he will. This is our ultimate hope in this broken world.

Riches of identity and inheritance

In Christ we not only *possess* an inheritance, we *are* an inheritance. We are God's inheritance—a chosen people for his own possession (1 Pet. 2:9). When Paul prays the Ephesian Christians will know "what are the riches of his glorious inheritance in the saints" (Eph. 1:18), commentators say he could either be referring to the inheritance believers possess, or the inheritance believers *are*. The original Greek allows for either interpretation.[7] Regardless of which Paul had in mind here, both are gloriously true. And the implications are huge! The fact that we are God's chosen inheritance means we are of inestimable value to him. We are precious to the God who made and redeemed us! As God's beloved daughters, we have also been given an inheritance that is beyond what we can imagine. We possess the many spiritual blessings of our new identity in Christ and the future riches of the life to come.

A woman who is truly secure in her identity and inheritance in Christ has great power. This woman is free from the nagging pressure to use her time and energy to prove her value, demand her rights, and promote herself. This woman is free from endless efforts to make a name for herself or amass earthly wealth. Because she is grounded in her true identity and inheritance, her gaze is transfixed on Christ rather than herself. He has satisfied her soul and given her the Holy Spirit, who is like rivers of living water flowing out of her heart (Jn. 7:38–39), empowering her to be poured out in service to others.

Greatness of an upside-down power

Society has proven women's ability to shatter glass ceilings, but it takes Spirit empowerment to quietly and joyfully lay down our lives for others each day. We've proven women possess the intellect and work ethic needed to be successful in practically any career, but no amount of female empowerment can protect us from calculating our worth by something as unstable as corporate success or financial security. Feminism has given us the illusion of complete control over our bodies, sexuality, and reproduction, but only the Spirit of God gives us self-control to deny gratifying every desire of the flesh. He alone helps us refuse to use beauty, immodesty, and sex appeal as sources of power over men, or to secure our own feelings of validation. It's the Holy Spirit who enables us to find comfort in the unpopular truth that real freedom is found only within God's good boundary lines.

Because Christian women are Spirit-empowered, we need not endlessly pursue worldly, female empowerment. The same power God worked when he raised Christ from the dead and seated him in heaven above all powers dwells in us (Eph. 1:20–21)! This is a mighty, upside-down, resurrection power by which we daily die to ourselves so that we may be raised to live for Christ and his glory. This is an end so much bigger and better than *us*. The indwelling Holy Spirit enables us to put to death remaining sin in our hearts and to battle the forces of evil that work to keep us blind, weak, self-absorbed, and fruitless. He equips us to carry out the good works God has prepared in advance for us to do in building his kingdom on earth (Eph. 2:10).

Summing it up

When I think back to the 2020 Super Bowl halftime show, I'm saddened that those superstars—those proud, provocative performers (and the many who laud them)—know nothing of true freedom and power. Are they beautiful and talented women? Without a doubt. Do they wield wide-spread influence because of their fame? Most definitely. But their lives proclaim the faux power of autonomy from God—a self-declared, self-rule that exposes, flaunts, demands, and seeks to control. Heartbreakingly, these women have not experienced the resurrection power that raises the dead and makes the truly repentant into new people. They know nothing of the power that quietly and mightily subverts the forces of evil—the power that enables believers to willingly lay down their lives in service to Christ, that they may be raised to eternal victory. They don't have eyes to see or hearts to experience the power that's making the whole world new. But we do. As women in Christ, we are indwelt by the Holy Spirit and are privy to his life-transforming, world-changing power every day. Sisters, we have something better than female empowerment. The Holy Spirit is the power we proclaim.

Questions for reflection and discussion

1. Have you ever felt confused about what *actually* empowers women? Jot down or discuss some ways the world defines female empowerment yet also sends confusing messages about it.

2. What is the only real basis for women's rights and all human rights? Why?

3. Many Christian women don't know what to think about the feminist movement. It appears to be a mixed bag of good (e.g. gaining women the right to vote) and bad (e.g. rejecting Christian sexual ethics). In what ways has the movement been harmful to women? In what ways has it failed to empower women? (Hint: Remember that power divorced from God is no power at all.)

4. Read John 14:16–17 and Ephesians 1:13–14. How does being sealed by the indwelling Holy Spirit empower us as women? (Hint: Remember the three purposes of a seal.)

5. Read Paul's prayer in Ephesians 1:16–19. What is he asking God to do for believers through the Holy Spirit? Explain how, biblically speaking, knowledge is power.

6. Paul prays the Spirit would enlighten believers to truly know the hope, riches, and power that are theirs in Christ. Read Ephesians 1:9–10. How does God's promise to unite all things in Christ bring us hope?

7. A woman who is secure in her identity and inheritance in Christ has great power. What is she free *from* and what is she free *for*?

8. Take some time to pray through Ephesians 1:16–19. Ask the Father to enlighten and empower you through his Spirit.

4
_____

Part of the Family

Belonging to Christ and each other

*But now in Christ Jesus you who once were far off have
been brought near by the blood of Christ. So then you are
no longer strangers and aliens, but you are fellow citizens
with the saints and members of the household of God.*
—*Ephesians 2:13, 19*

I will never forget the day a judge declared our fourth son
legally and officially part of our family forever. What a day of
celebration and rejoicing it was! What a huge sigh of relief we
breathed! We had waited, hoped, and prayed for Cameron's
adoption day for quite some time, and it had finally arrived.

Through events ordained by a sovereign God, Cameron
came to live with us when he was just three-and-a-half months
old—long before we adopted him. He came to us from painful,
broken circumstances, and from the moment he arrived in our
home, we loved him as our own. We cherished and cared for him
exactly as we did our three biological sons. And we prayed. First,
we pleaded with God to heal and restore Cameron's fractured

birth family. Second, we prayed that (if our first request was not God's sovereign will) he would make Cameron part of our family forever.

Any prospective adoptive parent will tell you they long for the day when the family ties are official. Whether a child has already come under their care, or they are waiting to see the child's face for the first time, those walking through the adoption process long for the day when the child shares their last name and legally belongs to them. Adoptive parents understand the vital importance of the child having family stability. Children need reliable, consistent caretakers and an unchanging group of people to call "home." They need a haven in which they are free and safe to be themselves—where they can love and be loved. Children need a place to truly belong, and they aren't the only ones.

It is not good to be alone

Virtually all secular psychologists agree that human relationships and a sense of belonging are important human needs. Many have developed theories to explain the reason for this need through the lens of evolution. Some posit that humans developed the need to belong to larger groups because it was essential for their survival. Living in community with others made it easier to find food and shelter, to ward off attacks from predators, and to reproduce and successfully raise offspring.[1]

As Christians who understand our origins through the lens of Scripture, we know that the human need for relationships and belonging derives from a greater source than our own frailty and fight for survival. The eternal Creator God is communal in his very essence and nature. In a mysterious union, God exists as three distinct persons—God the Father, God the Son, and God the Holy Spirit. These three persons of the Trinity live together in perfect fellowship, harmony, and love. Because God is relational in his very being, those made in his image are also relational. As humans, we were designed to live in open, joyful fellowship both with God and each other.

In the rhythmic six-day creation account of Genesis 1, God daily surveys his handiwork and six times declares it to be *good*. After forming humanity, the Creator looks back over the whole of his creation and declares it all to be *very good* (Gen. 1:31). Yet, in Genesis 2, God says for the first time that something is *not good*. After fashioning Adam from the dust of the ground and commissioning him to work and keep the garden, God said, "It is not good that the man should be alone; I will make him a helper fit for him" (Gen. 2:18). He then created Eve as Adam's perfect complement, and through their subsequent marriage union (Gen. 2:24–25), established the first family. God commissioned Adam and Eve to be fruitful and multiply—to have children, who would have children, who would have more children, and eventually populate the world (Gen. 1:28). This was God's *good* solution for Adam's *not good* aloneness.

The family—parents and children, grandparents, aunts and uncles, cousins, nieces, and nephews—has always been an important part of God's plan for human community and relationships at large. Families are the building blocks of whole societies, the most basic group in which a person should belong. New life should begin and grow within a family, and this is the first place where each individual should experience the joys of knowing and being known, loving and being loved. It's within families that humans should learn how to know God himself.

This plan for the family sounds quite lovely and rather idealistic, though, doesn't it?

Regardless of all the happy pictures posted on social media, no human family perfectly matches the ideal. Family is *hard*, and, heartbreakingly, families can fracture irreparably. This is one reason the adoption of children is necessary in the first place. Human families, intended to be safe havens of love and belonging, can inflict pain that leaves deep wounds, and it's quite possible to feel lonely, misunderstood, and not fully known within one's own family. Even the healthiest and most stable human families face the challenges and hardships of sinful people living life together, and they eventually face the separation death brings. For these reasons, it's crucial to remember that, while earthly family is important, it isn't ultimate. And a mom, dad, and 2.5 kids living together in a picturesque home with a white picket fence is not God's end goal for family. Our natural families were always intended to lead us to a greater reality.

Separation from God and each other

My dad and his four siblings recently sold their childhood home, "Camp Mt. Olive," a sprawling six-acre property in small-town Mississippi. The vast front yard was shaded by tall pecan trees and a giant oak. Flower and vegetable gardens, a pool, tennis court, hammock, playhouse, and giant tree swing all added to the grandeur of this childhood wonderland. Although my grandparents' home itself was hard to beat, it was really the people who made it so special. Camp Mt. Olive was the site of joyful family gatherings for years on end. It was the homeplace where a big family, spread around the southeastern US, returned several times each year for time together and a lot of good food, to boot. Losing Camp Mt. Olive felt almost as bad as losing my grandparents themselves because it was a stark reminder that even the best earthly families aren't forever. Eventually, separation is inevitable.

Separation is one of the most detrimental consequences of humanity's fall into sin. When Adam and Eve rebelled, they were first separated from God—exiled from the garden and his life-giving presence (Gen. 3:23–24). Sin created a dividing wall of hostility between God and humanity, which then led to numerous dividing lines between human beings. In this world, we not only experience the dissolution of family, but we also face the harsh reality of nations, people groups, and individuals at war with one another. The horrors of abandonment, divorce, and orphanhood are known to many. We experience rejection, cliquishness, and ostracism from various friendships and groups. Conflict and loneliness are universally experienced realities and, in many cases, leave catastrophic wreckage in their wake.

As human beings, we not only experience these divisions, we also cause them. While we may feel confident that we've not contributed to terrorism or world wars, have we not contributed to conflicts in our communities, neighborhoods, friendships, and families? Because of sin, disputes and division are natural, while harmony and unity are unnatural. And we are prone to building walls that exclude rather than opening doors to include. We form social cliques with those who look, think, and act like us, avoiding those who are different or with whom we might disagree. We curate our social media feeds into ideological echo chambers that cater to our personal preferences and beliefs, erecting fences based on political, theological, and sociological differences. We allow minor disagreement with others to quickly escalate, destroying valuable relationships in the process.

With so much division, it's no wonder loneliness is prevalent and we're all desperate to find the belonging we were designed for. No one wants to be alone, and no one is meant to be alone. Within every woman is a deep desire to draw near to others and find true *belonging*—to be part of something bigger than herself. But where can we possibly find it? If division and loneliness exist even in the best, God-ordained human relationships, what is the answer to this immense problem of separation? The short answer is the gospel.

Restoration plan: Old Testament Israel

You'll remember that the first ever family, Adam and Eve, were separated from God because of their rebellion against him. As the representative head of the entire human race, Adam plunged all of humanity into this same separation from their Creator. Yet, mercifully, God did not give up on his human children—and his restoration plan centered on a new family.

Years after Adam's and Eve's expulsion from the garden, God called a pagan man to leave his home and go to a new land. God blessed Abraham. He promised to give him numerous children, who would eventually form a great nation. God guaranteed that, through Abraham, all families of the earth would be blessed (Gen. 12:1–3). Abraham's offspring eventually formed the nation of Israel (Ex. 19:4–6). As a chosen people, the Israelites possessed benefits no other nations or peoples of the world enjoyed. They had access to God himself. God gave Israel the law to show them his holy character and teach them how to live in relationship with him. He gave them priests to serve as mediators between a holy God and sinful people. God's presence dwelt with Israel in the tabernacle and then the temple. He gave his people covenant promises, namely the promise of a coming Messiah who would give them eternal salvation and glory (Rom. 9:4).

God chose Israel to carry out his mission of restoration on earth. He granted them favor and "family benefits" so they could channel his blessing to the whole world. Israel was set apart to lead other nations and peoples out of separation and back into relationship with God. Sadly, though, they failed in this mission. The nation continually disobeyed God's law, breaking covenant with him and not living as his true children (Hos. 1:9). God's people went into exile—yet again separated from the One who called and redeemed them (Is. 5:5, 13). But even though Israel failed, God's restoration plan did not. You see, it was through the nation of Israel that Jesus the Messiah was born.

Mystery revealed: New Testament church

Have you ever felt a tinge of superiority because you're part of the "in group"? Or maybe you've experienced the sting of exclusion from a certain group you long to join. When Paul wrote to the church in Ephesus, he wrote in the context of deep racial tension between Jewish and Gentile (non-Jewish) believers. Jewish Christians felt superior because of the "family benefits" they had received as the old covenant people of God, whereas the Gentiles "were at that time separated from Christ, alienated from the commonwealth of Israel and strangers to the covenants of promise, having no hope and without God in the world" (Eph. 2:12). While not every ethnic Israelite had a saving relationship with God by faith (Rom. 9:6–8), to be an Israelite under the old covenant was to experience the general good of being in God's group. Israel possessed God's blessing, love, promises, and presence; thus, the citizens of this nation had (at the very least) *access* to the source of true hope. Gentiles, who did not have these advantages, were cut off from God's family and strangers to his promises. That is, until Christ's life, death, and resurrection changed everything.

As part of the original group, the Jews looked down on Gentile Christians who had not embraced the customs of Old Testament Judaism, such as circumcision. Paul explains how "the mystery of Christ"—once concealed but now revealed—reconciles these tensions (Eph. 3:4–5). By faith in Jesus' finished cross-work, both Jews *and* Gentiles become members of God's family, the church: "This mystery is that the Gentiles are fellow heirs, members of the same body, and partakers of the promise in Christ Jesus through the gospel" (Eph. 3:6). In other words, God's new "in group" includes both Jews and Gentiles who are *in Christ* by faith.

Earlier in the letter, Paul reminded the Gentiles just how much their status had changed:

> "But now in Christ Jesus you who once were far off have been brought near by the blood of Christ. For he himself is our peace, who has made us both one and has broken down in his flesh the dividing wall of hostility by abolishing the law of commandments expressed in ordinances, that he might create in himself one new man in place of the two, so making peace, and might reconcile us both to God in one body through the cross, thereby killing the hostility. And he came and preached peace to you who were far off and peace to those who were near. For through him we both have access in one Spirit to the Father" (Eph. 2:13–18).

When Jesus yielded up his Spirit on the cross, the curtain in the temple tore from top to bottom (Matt. 27:51). This torn veil, which had previously prohibited entrance into God's presence, now signaled that *all* sinners who trust Jesus by faith can draw near to God. Jesus' broken body broke down the barrier of separation between God and mankind. His shed blood made a way for people of all ethnicities to be restored to God as beloved sons and daughters. More than that, Christ's cross-work restores estranged human beings to one another by reconciling all who believe in one body called the church (Eph. 1:22–23, Eph. 2:16). Sin erects walls in human relationships, but Christ breaks them down, restoring the trinitarian-like union humans were created for. Theologian Gregg Allison says it this way: "Indeed, the church is a trinitarian re-creation: the people of God, the body of Christ, and the temple of the Holy Spirit."[2]

Part of the big invisible family

If you are in Christ, the reality of those early Christians, is your reality too:

> "So then you are no longer strangers and aliens, but you are fellow citizens with the saints and members of the household of God, built on the foundation of the apostles and prophets, Christ Jesus himself being the cornerstone, in whom the whole structure, being joined together, grows into a holy temple in the Lord. In him you also are being built together into a dwelling place for God by the Spirit" (Eph. 2:19–22).

As Christians, we not only belong to the Lord, but we also belong to his people. This is an impactful aspect of our identity. Once strangers, separated from God by sin, we are now members of his household—part of his "in group." Theologians call God's "household" the universal church, or "the community of all true believers for all time."[3] The universal church is made up of all redeemed image-bearers—women and men, girls and boys—from all generations and nationalities, for all of history. It is comprised of people in heaven (Heb. 12:22–23) and people on earth, all those God has restored to himself through Christ.

Members of God's household may have few commonalities apart from Christ, but *in him* they are spiritually united as one forever family. All members of this family across space and time are joined to the same Savior by a common faith, and all share the same Holy Spirit.[4] This means that Abraham, the Gentile Christians in Ephesus, the Apostle Paul, my grandparents, the elderly lady at the back of the church, the teenager who's just committed her life to Christ, you, me, and countless others are part of the same forever family. Ephesians 4:4–6 says, "There is one body and one Spirit—just as you were called to the one hope that belongs to your call—one Lord, one faith, one baptism, one God and Father of all, who is over all and through all and in all."

Consider this: If you are in Christ, you truly, deeply, eternally belong to a family that can never break. This family is indestructible because it is held together by a loving Father, who draws near to estranged children through his one sinless Son, sealing them as forever his by the Spirit. This reality doesn't change based on what you do, where you live, or where you go to church. Your true belonging in God's family doesn't fluctuate even when your *sense* of belonging does because of loneliness, interpersonal conflicts, or separation from others. You are an integral part of something bigger than yourself, and not even death can take this belonging from you.

In her book *A Place to Belong*, Megan Hill writes:

> *"God never intended that his people be isolated individuals. When we belong to Christ, we belong to a vast family that stretches all the way back to Adam and Noah and Abraham and all the way forward to the heavenly multitude that no one could number (Rev. 7:9). But our place in this family is not abstract or theoretical... We take our place in Christ's family by taking our place in the local church."*[5]

Part of the small visible family

Perhaps after reading the previous section, you're thinking, "What's so great about a giant family divided by space and time—a family I can't even see? How does this spiritual reality even begin to remedy all the conflict, separation, and isolation in my life and in the world today?" Or maybe you teeter toward the other end of the spectrum, and you're thinking, "I have a stable, happy nuclear family. We love Jesus, we love each other, and we're busy doing life together. I don't feel isolated right now. Sure, it's great that I'm part of the universal church, but I'm pretty satisfied with my own people."

Regardless of where you fall on this spectrum, you've likely heard someone say something like, "I have Jesus, and that's enough for me. I don't need the church; it's full of hypocrites anyway. I can't do organized religion." While the biblical truths I've communicated about the universal church may sound like metaphysical mumbo jumbo—too abstract to be of earthly good—we must remember that God has graciously made the invisible church *visible* through local churches.

A local church is a smaller, visible representation of the total community of the universal church. Local churches are familiar faces we can see, hands we can clasp, stomachs we can feed, and babies we can rock... all gathered together. Each local congregation, regardless of size, is a manifestation—a microcosm in one particular place and time—of the universal church.[6] When the New Testament authors wrote to specific local churches, they did not conceive of a person being *in Christ* without being an active member of a local fellowship. The Scriptures are clear: The unity we share with all believers in the universal church is to be lived out practically with a specific group of believers who make up a local congregation. To be *in Christ* is to be a part of his body, and to love Christ is to love his church in tangible ways.

In other words, because Christ has broken down the wall of separation and given us unshakeable belonging in God's family, we have both the duty and glorious privilege of living out that reality in a local context where God's Word is proclaimed. The people in our local church are *our* people—the ones with and to whom we belong. They are the ones with whom we get to worship, serve, pray, eat, fellowship, live in harmony, and practice the fifty some-odd "one another" commands of Scripture. The local church is where we are to know and be known, love and be loved.

Not yet perfected

As I type, I can already anticipate some of the questions and objections running through your mind. I anticipate them because

I've grappled with them myself. If the church is God's restored family, intended to manifest the reversal of sin's separation, why is family life in our churches still *so* hard? Unfortunately, we experience conflict, divisions, and loneliness in our local churches (just as the early churches did). Horrifyingly, some have even suffered abuse at the hands of someone within the church. The pain of these experiences and injustices is especially poignant because we *know* God intends for unity and love to characterize his family, and we know just how short we fall. Here, it's crucial to remember that the perfect spiritual unity we share within the universal church has not yet been perfected at the touch-and-see level in the local church. This is because individual, redeemed sinners have not yet been perfected. Although we are *in Christ*, we still struggle with remaining sin. In addition to the sin Christians bring, there are also wolves among the sheep within local churches (Acts 20:29–30). Some in our congregations sow destruction because they don't truly belong to Christ, and this reality will be revealed and judged when he returns (Matt. 25:31–33). But for all who *are* in Christ, a day is coming when our personal righteousness and, thereby, our practical unity will be perfected.[7] For now, we must hope, pray, and work for what we do not yet see, waiting for it with patience (Rom. 8:24–25).

And as we wait, we get to live into this glorious reality within our local churches right now, albeit imperfectly. Maybe you wish your church lived more like the first-century church, sharing daily life and material goods regularly (Acts 2:42–47). Maybe you wish community life wasn't so messy and that Christians weren't still so prone to controversy. Maybe you long to experience greater *feelings* of belonging and wish your church family could totally eradicate the loneliness that plagues you.

These aren't necessarily bad longings; they point to the perfect sense of belonging we will experience when Christ's kingdom comes in fullness on earth. In the meantime, let's be careful not to idolize the heavenly ideal at the expense of the brothers and sisters God has given us to love and serve today. Christ loves the church for whom he died—the church he will one day present to himself "without spot or wrinkle or any such thing" (Eph. 5:27). So, we too must love her as she is right now. We love the church by *being* the church—by being "eager to maintain the unity of the Spirit in the bond of peace" (Eph. 4:3) as we selflessly serve one another.

So, look for the person sitting alone next Sunday morning, and go say hello. Send the text. Take the meal. Open your home and table often. Serve in the nursery. Start the ministry where you see a void. Pray for your brothers and sisters. Commit to your local fellowship, and don't church hop at the first sign of trouble. Family life in the local church will never be easy or totally fulfilling this side of eternity. But the imperfections don't change the beautiful reality God has established or make it any less glorious. You were once far off, but Christ brought you near to God and his people! Joy will come as you participate in that reality.

Summing it up

Soon after Cameron came to live with us, I began to pray that God would officially bring him into our family forever. But I didn't end my prayer there. The following words are scribbled in my prayer journal frequently: "Lord, make him part of our family, but more importantly, please make him part of *your* family forever." Cameron needs an earthly family, but we are not his hope for salvation and true restoration. We cannot reconcile and restore him to the God he so desperately needs. Regardless of how well we love him in this life, we cannot give him true belonging in an everlasting family that even death can't break. Only Jesus can do that for him, and only Jesus can do that for you and me. In Christ, we are members of God's forever family, and nothing can separate us from his love.

Questions for reflection and discussion

1. Why do all human beings need and want to belong to a group bigger than themselves? Based on Genesis 2:5–25, explain how the family was a fundamental part of God's plan for human community and relationships at large. What went wrong?

2. How have you seen sin's separating effects in the world? How have you experienced sin's separating effects in your own life?

3. What part was Israel supposed to play in God's plan to restore people back to himself and to each other? How did Israel fail? Why did God's plan succeed despite Israel's failure?

4. What is the mystery Paul seeks to convey in Ephesians 2:11–22? How does the cross-work of Christ eradicate the separation that sin caused between God and mankind? And between people?

5. If you are in Christ, you belong to God's unbreakable, eternal family. How does this bring you comfort and joy while you are still living in a world full of conflict, separation, and loneliness?

6. Our local churches are not yet perfectly united. Why is this? How does Ephesians 5:27 encourage us about the future?

7. Are you an active, serving member of a local church? What are some practical ways you can seek to be the church to others in your local body, especially to those with whom you may differ or disagree?

5

Walking Worthy

How identity in Christ drives activity for Christ

Walk in a manner worthy of the calling to which you have been called... put off your old self, which belongs to your former manner of life and is corrupt through deceitful desires... put on the new self, created after the likeness of God in true righteousness and holiness.
—Ephesians 4:1, 22, 24

I was a young child sitting in the small study of my family's newly built home when I heard the gospel for the first time. My dad, a physician, had just returned from a medical mission trip to Central America. Using an old-school slide projector, he cast photos on an empty wall of the home office as he told our family all about his trip. Looking directly at me and my siblings, he said, "While it's true that I went to give the people of Nicaragua medicines to help their bodies get well, those medicines won't last long. Their bodies will eventually get sick again, and one day they will die. I really went on this trip to give them something better than medicine—something that can heal them forever."

Dad went on to explain the universal problem of sin and the good news of the gospel—just as he had shared it with the Nicaraguan people. That night as he spoke, I understood the grave reality of my own sin against God and my deep need for a Savior. In the simple words of a child, I repented of my sin and put my faith in Jesus Christ, trusting him alone for forgiveness. Although I was young, I believe it was that very night with my family in our home office that the Spirit of God awakened my heart and brought me from spiritual death to life in Christ (Eph. 2:4–5). From that point on, I began to grow in my knowledge of and love for the Lord.

By this, I am not saying that living the Christian life was all smooth sailing, or that I ceased to struggle with sin. Of course not! In fact, while I realized from an early age that the gospel is good news for my eternal destiny, it was many, many years before I fully understood that the gospel is also good news for my life *today*. For a long time, I saw the good news of Jesus' life, death, and resurrection simply as the entryway to salvation, and I functioned as if spiritual growth and the fight against remaining sin were pretty much up to me to accomplish by my own willpower and strength. Maybe I'm not the only one?

Pastor J.D. Greear writes:

> *"For many of us the gospel functions solely as the entry rite into Christianity... The gospel, however, is not just the diving board off of which we jump into the pool of Christianity; it is the pool itself. It is not only the way we begin in Christ; it is the way we grow up in Christ... That's why growth in Christ is never going beyond the gospel but going deeper into the gospel."*[1]

In other words, the gospel is not just the door we walk through to get on the pathway to heaven. Rather, it's the good news that affects every facet of our lives and womanhood right now.

Identity drives activity

I've found that one of the greatest challenges of being an author is living what I write. It's fairly easy for me to learn biblical truth and put it into words on the page. The real test comes when I must get up from the keyboard and act on the truths I've written about. This is where the rubber meets the road. It's the turning point—the place where I find out if I really believe what I claim to believe. In a similar way, Ephesians 4 is a turning point in the letter. In the first three chapters of the epistle, Paul explains what God has accomplished for those who are in Christ. He details the Christian's new identity and benefits. At the beginning of chapter 4, the Apostle makes a shift. He moves from explaining what has already been accomplished for believers and calls them to obedient action as a result. Paul writes, "I therefore, a prisoner for the Lord, urge you to walk in a manner worthy of the calling to which you have been called" (Eph. 4:1). This transition from positional truth (what God has done) to practical truth (how we should live as a result) is a common pattern in Paul's letters.

Before attempting to understand what it means to "walk worthy" of our calling, we need to highlight a crucial word in Ephesians 4:1: *therefore*. Bible teachers often quip, "When you see the word *therefore*, you need to ask yourself what it's *there for*." It's true! The word therefore is like a flashing sign, calling readers to remember what was written previously in order to understand what will come next. Through this transitional word, Paul exhorts his audience to read, interpret, and apply all he is about to write through the lens of what he has written thus far. He wants believers to understand two things before moving forward. First, God's work *in* us demands an active response *from* us. Second, our obedience must flow from deep trust in what the Father has already accomplished for us through his Son. The two are never disconnected and must never be reversed. Wholly resting in Christ leads to a lifestyle of committed obedience to him. Said another way, our identity in Christ (to which we contribute nothing) drives our activity for Christ (which involves our effort).

The worthy walk

So, what does Paul mean when he commands believers to walk in a manner worthy of their calling? The Greek word translated *worthy* in this passage means to balance the scales.[2] Picture the old-fashioned scales of justice you might see in a lawyer's office. The weight on one scale must match the weight on the other scale for the two to properly balance. Or perhaps think of a seesaw. When my son Luke was small, he often asked me to play on the seesaws with him at a particular park. This never worked well because I was so much larger than him. Instead of the long plank teetering up and down, our disproportionate weight meant that my side stayed on the ground while his side stayed in the air. The imbalance rendered the seesaw ineffective (and highly frustrating to Luke). I explained to him that the weight on each side needed to be a closer match for the seesaw to work properly.

In a similar way, Paul's instruction to "walk worthy" is a call to let our lifestyle match our high position in Christ. As Christian women, there should be equilibrium between *who* we are and *how* we live. One commentator says it this way: "Because God has set his hand upon us and called us, changing us from what we were into what we have now become, we are to live as Christians in this world."[3] This is a common theme throughout the Scriptures. Before God gave Israel his law to obey, he reminded them of their identity as his chosen and redeemed people (Ex. 20:2). John the Baptist commanded those who had publicly repented of their sins to "bear fruits in keeping with repentance" (Lk. 3:8). Jesus himself taught that a person's true identity is evidenced by how she lives her life: "For no good tree bears bad fruit, nor again does a bad tree bear good fruit, for each tree is known by its own fruit" (Lk. 6:43–44). James taught that true faith is accompanied by good works: "What good is it, my brothers, if someone says he has faith but does not have works? Can that faith save him? So also faith by itself, if it does not have works, is dead" (Jas. 2:14, 17).

We know from these multiple commands in Scripture, and from our own consciences, that we should live in ways that reflect our identity in Christ. But we also know, quite painfully, that this is easier said than done. When we snap at our children, gossip with a sister at church, complain about our circumstances, wallow in self-pity, make selfish demands of our spouse, or succumb to anger, vanity, laziness, or lust, we feel the disconnect. It's disheartening to see just how short we fall, isn't it? The unbalanced scales of who we are in Christ compared to our attitudes and actions in day-to-day life typically lead us to strive harder to be good in our own strength. Alternatively, the imbalance leaves us feeling discouraged and possibly questioning our salvation. Is this what the Christian life is supposed to be like? Either constantly attempting to pull ourselves up by our own bootstraps, or wondering if we're even really saved? Is it possible that the gospel could not only affect our eternal destiny but also empower our fruitful obedience today? In order to answer these questions, we need to make sure we understand salvation as the Bible presents it—a unity of past, present, and future aspects.

Salvation past

When did you get saved? This was a common question among my church-going peers during our youth group days. As a teenager, if someone asked me when I "got saved," I thought back to that time as a young child when I responded to the message of the gospel, asking Jesus to forgive my sins and be my Lord. Many of us have probably either asked or been asked the same question and are, therefore, familiar with language that speaks of salvation (for current believers) as a past event.

Of course, salvation past is not simply the time a sinner "prayed a prayer." Salvation past is a work of God, who, by his grace alone, made the spiritually dead sinner alive in Christ (theologians call this regeneration). She then responded to hearing the gospel message by turning away from sin and putting her faith in Jesus (theologians call this conversion). God then instantaneously forgave her of all sins past, present, and future, legally declaring her to be righteous before him (theologians call this justification).

Salvation past is a once-for-all, irrevocable act of God accomplished apart from any effort or merit in the person being saved. When people refer to the time they "got saved," they are often thinking of justification (even if they don't know the theological word) because it's by justification that sinners are pardoned from the eternal punishment their sins deserve.

Justification is a legal declaration made by God—imagine a judge slamming down a gavel and declaring the defendant "not guilty." God remains perfectly just in declaring a person "not guilty" before him because of all Jesus achieved on her behalf. He credits the perfect righteousness of Christ to the believer's spiritual account.

That night so many years ago in my family's home office, I *was* saved—made spiritually alive, fully forgiven, declared guiltless, and bound for heaven. It was at that time that my identity in Christ was sealed forever by the Holy Spirit. All of this was a gift of God to which I contributed nothing (Eph. 2:8–9) and, therefore, cannot lose. But the Scriptures teach that I have not only *been saved* in the past, but I am also *being saved* in the present (1 Cor. 1:18; 1 Cor. 15:2), and I *will be saved* in the future (Rom. 8:30).

Salvation present and future

Francis Schaeffer explains, "Salvation is not just justification and then a blank until death; God never meant it to be so. Salvation is a unity, a flowing stream from justification through sanctification to glorification."[4] Sanctification is just another big theological word referring to the believer's gradual growth in Christ-likeness; her progress in walking worthy of her calling. We understand what progressive growth looks like physically. When a baby girl is born, she possesses the necessary organs and body parts to eventually become a woman. But an infant doesn't go to bed one night and wake up the next morning fully grown. Growth and maturation happen over a period of years through a lot of nurture. Sanctification is similar in its progressive nature. We don't wake up perfectly loving, joyful, peaceful, patient, and kind the morning after we are justified. These fruits of the Spirit, among many others, are cultivated and grow over time.

It's crucial to grasp some important distinctions between justification and sanctification if we are to rightly understand the relationship between God's grace and our works. While justification is salvation *past*, sanctification is salvation *present* and involves the believer's on-going relationship with Christ today. In justification, sinners are immediately set free from the *penalty* of sin for all eternity; through sanctification, sinners are gradually set free from the *practice* of sin in their daily lives (because sin has lost its controlling power over them). While justification is instantaneous, sanctification is gradual over the course of a person's whole Christian life on earth. Justification is a work of God alone, but sanctification is a work in which God and the believer cooperate (Phil. 2:12). In justification, the believer's righteous *position* before God is secured forever; in sanctification, the believer's righteous *practice* is slowly but surely increasing. In justification, the believer receives a new identity *in* Christ. In sanctification, the believer is learning to live *for* Christ.

Salvation future is called *glorification* and will happen when Christ returns to earth, raises the dead, and gives his people resurrected bodies devoid of sin and suffering. At that point, we won't only have been saved from the penalty and power of sin, but we'll also be saved from the very presence of sin forever! I was in my early twenties as a seminary student before I clearly grasped the unity and distinctions between salvation past, present, and future. Salvation is a unity of justification, sanctification, and glorification because all three are connected in one unbreakable chain and empowered by the same grace. If God has declared you righteous in his sight, you can know with certainty that he will progressively make you righteous until you are perfected on the day of his return (Rom. 8:30). Regardless of how long and messy the process is, God promises to finish the good work he begins in every true believer (Phil. 1:6). This is so important to understand because sometimes growth in Christ can feel like one step forward and two steps back.

As a teenager, I was actively involved in the youth group at church and was there almost anytime the doors opened. However, I don't recall ever being taught about salvation as a unity of past, present, and future aspects. This explains some of the patterns and struggles I saw in myself and other church kids at the time. Some teens believed that because they had prayed the prayer of salvation and been baptized, they were automatically bound for heaven, regardless of how they lived. They didn't take growth in Christ seriously. Other kids struggled under the discouragement and shame of remaining sin in their lives, wondering why they kept giving in to temptation if they were truly saved. These students kept their sin hidden and lacked assurance of salvation. Some even made repeated professions of faith or kept rededicating their lives to Christ to gain a sense of assurance.

Like the kids in my former youth group, too many Christian women do not understand the unity and distinctions of salvation past, present, and future. When these theological waters get muddied in people's minds, problems arise. For instance, let's say thirty-year-old Sally is confused about justification. Because she doesn't understand that God declares sinners righteous by faith in Jesus alone, she continually strives to be good enough to keep God pleased with her. She works hard to be the perfect wife, mom, church member, and friend. She reads her Bible daily, serves in multiple areas at church, and generally goes above and beyond in every area of life. When she sins, she immediately thinks God is angry and wants to punish her. As a result, her prayer life has become practically non-existent, and she keeps her struggles hidden. Sally is trusting in her good works rather than resting in Christ by faith.

On the other hand, let's say thirty-year-old Mary has little time or desire for the things of the Lord. She prayed the prayer of salvation as a child at a Vacation Bible School many years ago (and believes "once saved, always saved"), but the Bible seems too hard to understand, prayer is boring, and church attendance is a low priority. Mary is irritated by the constant demands of raising small children and finds herself frequently flying off the handle. At night, she drinks wine to take the edge off while binge-watching Netflix and hoping she can make it through another day. She feels like a failure and wonders why she can't get it together and feel more joy, especially if she's a Christian. Mary doesn't recognize that God has called her to actively participate in her growth in Christ. She makes little effort to practice the spiritual disciplines yet wonders why God doesn't just change her.

Like Sally, if we don't understand that justification is an instantaneous, one-time declaration of God based on our faith in Jesus alone, each fall into sin will leave us doubting we are forever forgiven and loved by him. On the other hand, if, like Mary, we fail to recognize that sanctification is an on-going work of grace in our lives that we're called to participate in, we will feel apathetic and discouraged when growth in practical righteousness seems too slow to even be measurable.

As a teen, I understood that God had forgiven me through Jesus, sparing me from the eternal punishment my sins deserved. What I didn't yet understand was how this past reality affected my life and spiritual growth in the present. In other words, I didn't understand how my justification, sanctification, and eventual glorification are all connected and accomplished by the same grace. It was clear to me that I should go to church, read my Bible, pray, be kind to people, obey my parents, remain sexually pure, and try to be a generally upstanding, moral person. After all, that's what the Bible says Christians *should* do, and since my personality tends toward people-pleasing and rule-following, I tried hard. But the Christian life isn't a pull-yourself-up-by-your-own-bootstraps-and-try-harder life. We're not saved by God's grace and then left alone to be good in our own strength (Gal. 3:3). Yes, we are called to actively participate in our spiritual growth, but our efforts are to be grace-driven and Spirit-empowered. The same grace that justified us will also sanctify us—God has promised it (Rom. 8:29–30)! As a teenager, I needed to grow in my understanding of this reality: True obedience *to* Christ is fueled by resting *in* Christ—by becoming rooted and grounded in his love.

What part do we play?

The Scriptures teach that sanctification is a work in which both God and the believer cooperate (Phil. 2:12–13), but this begs some questions: What part does God play, and what part do we play? How do we participate in our spiritual growth without falling into self-sufficient striving (Gal. 3:3) and then despairing when we fail? The answers to these questions are revealed in Paul's prayer at the end of Ephesians 3.

Immediately before the command to "walk worthy" (Eph. 4:1), Paul prays for the Ephesian Church. He pleads with God to strengthen their faith by grounding them in the love of Christ:

83

> "...may [they] have strength to comprehend with all the saints what is the breadth and length and height and depth, and to know the love of Christ that surpasses knowledge, that [they] may be filled with all the fullness of God" (Eph. 3:18–19).

He then asks God to glorify himself by working powerfully within the church, doing "far more abundantly than all that we ask or think" (Eph. 3:20). So, before Paul gives any commands for how to live, he wants believers to understand that it's *God's* power through the Holy Spirit that ultimately sanctifies believers. The Spirit empowers change in our lives by enabling us to *know* the love of Christ in a deep, saving way that far surpasses head knowledge. Becoming deeply rooted in Christ's love is what propels us to repeatedly turn away from sin and live for him. In other words, the gospel of grace, rather than striving in our own strength, enables continual repentance and spiritual growth.

I enjoy any chance to change out of my typical "mom wardrobe" of athletic wear and get dressed up to go somewhere. In Ephesians 4, Paul describes repentance (a change of mind leading to a change of direction) with language indicative of a wardrobe change:

> "...put off your old self, which belongs to your former manner of life and is corrupt through deceitful desires, and... be renewed in the spirit of your minds, and... put on the new self, created after the likeness of God in true righteousness and holiness" (Eph. 4:22–24).

Just like we might take off sweaty leggings after a run, Christians are commanded to intentionally take off the sinful deeds that characterized our lives before Christ and "put on" righteous deeds in their place. We are to put off falsehood and put on truth (Eph. 4:25), put off stealing and put on honest labor and generous giving (Eph. 4:28), put off corrupting talk and put on uplifting speech (Eph. 4:29). Pastor Kent Butterfield explains, "We are going from old to new, putting off and putting on. This is the constant spiritual activity of the child of God who is living a repentant life."[5] Although this putting off and putting on requires on-going effort, we must remember that it is accomplished only by God's enabling grace through the power of the Spirit.

Perhaps a hypothetical story will help bring this to life. Imagine that you, a commoner, marry the heir to the throne. You are greatly loved, not only by your new husband but also by his father, the king himself. As a new member of the royal family, you are expected to dress a certain way—a way that rightly reflects your identity and honors your position as future queen. While a hoodie and sweatpants might feel most natural and comfortable, you certainly wouldn't appear at a state dinner in loungewear! Dressing poorly wouldn't alter your identity or your new family's love for you but, *because* you love and desire to honor them, you would seek to dress—not just appropriately—but beautifully.

In the same way, when you truly *know* who you are because of God's grace—when you are awed and humbled because of the new position, glorious identity, and forever love God has bestowed on you in his Son—you will desire to dress the part! And the same grace that already covered you in the righteousness of Christ will enable you to put on the beautiful garments of godly living each day.

It's crucial to understand that Paul is not advocating for moralism (the attempt to earn God's favor by being good) in his command to "put off" and "put on." The Apostle isn't wagging his finger at us saying, "You better straighten up and fly right!" No, Paul is simply calling us to live in accordance with our identity. We do this by pursuing obedience as we lean into his transforming grace. Commentator James Montgomery Boice writes:

> "The apostle is not merely urging a new higher standard of morality on people. That is an utterly futile thing... Rather, Paul is demanding a high form of behavior precisely because something decisive has already taken place. We have already been made new in Christ. That is why we should and must act like it."[6]

In *Every Moment Holy*, Douglas McKelvey beautifully captures the tension of grace-driven effort in the sanctification process. After reminding us of God's command to love him with all our hearts, souls, minds, and strength (Lk. 10:27), and then listing ways we should demonstrate this love, he prompts us to consider: "Do you now possess the strength to accomplish such holy requirements?" And of course, "We do not," but wonderfully that's not the entirety of the answer:

> "We do not. We are weak and inconsistent, and often buffeted by fear and pride and selfishness. But being impoverished and ill-equipped as we are, we will look to the grace of God

and to the sanctifying work of the Spirit to accomplish
his purposes in and through us this day, as we, in grateful
response, seek to choose that which pleases him."[7]

Summing it up

Not too long after the night Christ saved me in my family's home
office, I started writing about my faith. Through the years, I've
filled numerous journals with prayers and musings about what
God is showing me in his Word. While I've always loved to write,
it wasn't until my mid-twenties that I shared any of that writing
publicly by starting a blog. As I finished up my seminary degree,
I wanted a space not only to work out what I was learning but
also to communicate truth and hope to others. Coming up with a
title for the blog was a challenge but, after a few tries, I eventually
landed on *Gospel-Shaped Womanhood*. During that season of life,
the Holy Spirit brought so much to light for me. Although I had
been a Christian for many years, it was *then* that I really grasped
how the gospel is good news affecting not only my eternal destiny
but also shaping every aspect of my life and womanhood in the
present. As someone prone to strive in my own strength, I began
to gain clarity about the relationship between grace and works, as
well as the unity and distinctiveness of salvation past, present, and
future. Through solid biblical teaching and theological training,
God opened my eyes to see how Jesus' finished work has powerful
implications for every practical part of my life, from my work to
my relationships to my trials. I realized that becoming deeply
rooted in my *identity* in Christ is what would fuel God-glorifying
activity for Christ. And I finally began to see that the work of
participating in my sanctification must flow from wholly resting
in what God has already accomplished in my justification. It was

because I so desperately wanted to share this life-changing good news with other women that many blog articles, Instagram posts, and even the idea for this book were born. The gospel is truly for all of life, and I can't wait to explore that reality with you in the pages ahead.

Questions for reflection and discussion

1. If someone asked when you got saved, what would you say? Share your story of salvation past.

2. "The gospel… is not only the way we begin in Christ; it is the way we grow up in Christ" (J.D. Greear). Is this concept new to you? Based on what you've read in this chapter, what does this mean?

3. Read Ephesians 4:1 and describe the shift Paul makes at this point in his letter. Why is "therefore" a crucial word in 4:1?

4. Explain what Paul means when he urges believers to walk worthy of their calling (Eph. 4:1). What wrong ways of thinking and acting are we prone to when we realize this is easier said than done?

5. What are the theological words for salvation past, present, and future? Discuss or jot down some of the distinctions between these three. Describe how they are also an unbreakable unity (see Rom. 8:29–30). As you look at your own life, how do both realities bring you comfort?

6. As Christian women, what part do we play in our own sanctification (Eph. 4:20–24)? How is this different from striving harder to be good in our own strength?

7. "Identity drives activity." Explain what is meant by this statement. What are some practical ways you can seek to become deeply rooted in Christ in order to spur godly living?

Part 2:

GOSPEL-SHAPED ACTIVITY

Ephesians 4 – 6

6

Women Who Work

Nurturing life for the glory of God

For we are his workmanship, created in Christ Jesus
for good works, which God prepared beforehand, that
we should walk in them.
—Ephesians 2:10

But grace was given to each one of us according
to the measure of Christ's gift.
—Ephesians 4:7

"Do you get paid for any of the work you do?" A friend posed the question to me as we watched our children ride their scooters around the church gym, squealing with delight. I was caught off-guard and pleasantly surprised by her unusual choice of words. "Do you work?" is a more typical rendering of the same inquiry. And while often asked innocently to distinguish between paid and unpaid work, the wording seems to imply some women are workers and others are not.

At the time, the answer to my friend's question was no. I was busy raising three little boys, managing our home, and helping my husband in ministry. I was also counseling several women through a local non-profit, leading a small group women's Bible study, and teaching in the children's ministry at church. While none of this was paid work, it was all *real* work, nonetheless, and I was grateful that my friend acknowledged that reality.

As women, can anything make us feel more insecure than being asked "What do you do?"? Whether we're caring for children, working a nine-to-five, volunteering in the church or community, managing a household (plus or minus a side hustle), or attempting to do some combination of these things, we often wonder if the work we do is truly meaningful. Does it count as *real* work if it's unpaid? Are our labors making any difference in the world, or at least in the lives of those around us? Have we worked hard enough even if no one sees evidence of it? Do the seemingly mundane tasks between the punch-in and punch-out each day have value and significance beyond a paycheck?

Even as Christians, we are prone to evaluate our work based on what the world says a successful woman should do. The comparison and striving to prove ourselves (even if only *to ourselves*) can feel endless, and the satisfaction of "success" is often short-lived or altogether elusive. As women who are *in Christ*, we must learn to evaluate our work through the lens of the gospel. Here are some questions to consider: Do I understand God's purpose for human work? Am I using God's standard to measure success? How does a gospel-shaped identity affect the way I understand and carry out my work?

Created to work

For our view of work to be shaped by the gospel, we must go back to the beginning of the Bible's story—to the time when work began. Work is introduced in the opening pages of Scripture where we read about God's work of creation, and his work-mandate to the first human beings: "Be fruitful and multiply and fill the earth and subdue it" (Gen. 1:28). In going back to the beginning, the first important thing to note is this: Work was not a result of humanity's fall into sin; rather, it was part of God's original, good plan for those made in his image. Work is a creation ordinance, essential for human life and flourishing. God made us to work, and our work as service to him is good and purposeful. From the beginning, humans were given the joyful task of representing God in the world. They were commissioned to expand, cultivate, and care for his creation in ways that would propagate his glory to every corner of the earth. Both the man and the woman were created for fruitful labor.

Adam was made first, but he was not equipped to carry out God's commission alone. Adam could not "be fruitful and multiply" by himself. He needed someone to complement him—someone who shared his humanity yet differed from him—to help fill and subdue the earth. So, God created the woman. She was made uniquely female and, even *after* her willful rebellion, graciously given the name Eve, which means "the mother of all living" (Gen. 3:20). What was meant to be fulfilling labor for humanity became hard toil after sin entered the world, but Eve (and her future daughters) were still granted the glorious privilege of carrying out life-giving work.

Distorted relationship with work

Isn't it interesting how it is ingrained in us from a young age that identity is wrapped up in vocation? Young children are not typically asked what they want to *do* when they grow up; they are usually asked what they want to *be*. *Do you want to be a teacher? A policeman? A doctor? A nurse?* While these titles are helpful ways of describing the regular work someone has been trained to do, they also reveal the human tendency to link who we are to our work. Professions have become identities, particularly in affluent Western culture where education is a relatively accessible commodity. By the time children become teenagers, they learn that pursuing certain vocations—typically those that require more education and lead to bigger paychecks—could elevate their status as persons in the eyes of the world. As a result, many young people end up pursuing work that isn't suited to their natural abilities and interests.

This is a fundamentally broken way of understanding work, and it leads to all sorts of problems. While work is, in large part, what humans are here on earth to *do*, it is not who we *are*. From creation, human work was meant to be the joyful overflow of an identity firmly rooted in God and tethered to the ultimate purpose of bringing him glory by fulfilling his plan in the world. Work was never primarily about *us*—our fulfillment, our self-actualization, our worth. We were meant to find those things in relationship with God *while* carrying out the good work he has given us to do. When sin severed us from our Creator, the true purpose of work was distorted in our minds and hearts. No longer secure as beloved children of God, we now seek to find worth in what we can accomplish and achieve instead. This isn't new, but it's dangerous. Remember how some of the earliest people tried to build a city and tower to heaven to make a name for themselves (Gen. 11:1–9)?

Here's the truth: Human identity rooted in anything other than God himself is idolatry. Anything we look to apart from God for our ultimate sense of worth is an idol. Work was meant to be a means of worshiping God and fulfilling his mission of love, but it so easily becomes a channel for self-worship (if we think we've succeeded) or despair (if we think we've failed). The same hissing voice Eve heard in the garden so many years ago whispers to us that we need not rest in God's love and work for *his* glory. We can go our own way and pursue a glory that's all our own: *Chase your dreams! Climb the ladder! Build your platform! Get more followers! Make good money! Pursue security and comfort first and foremost. And, by all means, make a name for yourself!* While we may not all pursue the things on that list, we all naturally work for our own renown rather than God's.

But idolizing work leads to real misery. It's at the root of why we sometimes feel insecure about what we do. It's why the stay-at-home mom ponders if she should get a "real job," while the single woman working nine-to-five wonders if her labors will have lasting significance. It's why we struggle with discontent when we look around and compare how we spend our days to how other women spend theirs. It's why we feel despair when someone else gets the job instead of us and why we beat ourselves up when we haven't been as productive as we wanted to be on any certain day. It's why we easily fall into workaholism and the obsessive drive to do more, more, more. And it's why we're often blind to the value of labor that is mundane, inefficient, and not applauded by the world around us. We long for our work to make us a *somebody*, but even the best jobs can't carry the weight of our identity.

Recreated for good works

One of the first passages of Scripture I memorized as a child was Ephesians 2:8–9:

> *"For by grace you have been saved through faith. And this is not your own doing; it is the gift of God, not a result of works, so that no one may boast."*

These well-known verses summarize the heart of the gospel, but they are first like a cup of ice-cold water to the face—a humbling jolt to remind us that we've never been self-sufficient and can never work hard enough to earn God's favor. God's love and salvation are free gifts of his grace that must be received. Ephesians 2:8–9 is a painful blow to the pride of those who idolize self and work because these verses require us to acknowledge that we are broken by sin and helpless to meet our most fundamental human need—forgiveness and a restored relationship with our Creator. We have no cause to boast, which stings until we read the following verse:

> *"For we are his workmanship, created in Christ Jesus for good works, which God prepared beforehand that we should walk in them"* (Eph. 2:10).

While we cannot work to earn what we need most, the good news of the gospel is that Jesus did the work *for us*. Because of the cross, God does a work of re-creation *in* us by his grace. We are his workmanship or masterpiece (as some Bible translations put it). We've been made into new people through our union with Christ, so we can carry out the good works

98

God prepared for us to do—including our normal, everyday jobs! This is amazingly good news to women whose view and practice of labor is distorted by idolatry. When God grants us identity in Christ, he also begins to progressively redeem our relationship with work. In his book *Every Good Endeavor*, Tim Keller writes:

> "*The gospel frees us from the relentless pressure of having to prove ourselves and secure our identity through work, for we are already proven and secure... All work now becomes a way to love the God who saved us freely; and by extension, a way to love our neighbor.*"[1]

Secular or sacred work?

So, what does this look like at a practical level? What *are* the good works God prepared for women to do here on earth? Unfortunately, when thinking about Ephesians 2:10, we're often prone to draw some sacred/secular divisions. For instance, things like feeding the homeless at a soup kitchen, reading our Bibles and praying, teaching Sunday school, or going on a mission trip seem to be the type of good works Paul is talking about. These are "churchy" things after all. But what about faithfully working an ordinary job day in and day out? What about the labors of making and keeping a home where others are fed, clothed, and loved? What about planting a garden or preparing a delicious meal? What about the creative work of writing music, poetry, and books, or the innovative and technical work of building airplanes, houses, and washing machines? What about the work of making lesson plans to teach children or seeing patients each day in a medical clinic?

I think it's common, even for believers, to consider the first list of works "sacred" and the second list "secular" and, thus, not connected to our spiritual lives. But for those in Christ, there is really no split. Whether it's paid employment or unpaid service, *all* work is a means to seek first God's kingdom and glory, rather than our own. *All* work is an opportunity to love God and others as we subdue and cultivate the world he has given us to steward. According to the famous reformer Martin Luther:

> "*Every occupation has its own honor before God. Ordinary work is a divine vocation or calling. In our daily work, no matter how important or mundane, we serve God by serving the neighbor, and we also participate in God's on-going providence for the human race.*"[2]

Paul reminds believers that we are "bondservants of Christ" and should, therefore, make every effort to carry out "the will of God from the heart" in our work (Eph. 6:6). Regardless of what we do, we are to "[render] service with a good will as to the Lord and not to man" (Eph. 6:7). There isn't necessarily a "one-size-fits-all" mold when it comes to the work of women. While the motivation and purpose underlying a Christian woman's work should never change, the type of work each of us does will likely look different, particularly in various seasons and stages of life. The work of the single mother will differ from the work of the married woman without children. The work of the college student will differ from the work of a woman in her sixties, but the ultimate motivation for our work is the same. There are innumerable ways to use our gifts, talents, education, and resources to glorify God as we cultivate and enhance life in his world. Remembering that our identity is in Christ, not in our vocation, enables us to labor for the Lord from a right heart, taking our cues from the Word rather than the world.

Life-givers in the home

When I was born, my mom left behind a prestigious career and high salary in order to stay at home with me and (later) my siblings. During my eighteen years at home—and far beyond that time—I watched as she skillfully wielded her sharp intellect, talents, and gifts to care for our family and cultivate our home into a warm and inviting haven for us and for others. My mom tirelessly invested in her children's growth and well-being in countless ways. She nurtured us through hot meals, ironed clothes, prayers, quality time, wise counsel, gifts, biblical teaching, and intentional involvement in our lives. She planned birthday parties, traveled to hundreds of sporting events, proofread our papers for English, and tutored us (and our friends) in math. When my siblings and I were teenagers, our house was often the place where our friends wanted to hang out. Our back door was unlocked, our kitchen was clean and inviting, and our pantry was full of snacks because my mother lovingly and sacrificially gave herself to the work of home and family. The fruit of her labors is incalculable. Despite this, I recall a friend once asking, "So, what does your mom do all day since she doesn't work?" The question seemed so silly and ignorant since my mother was, quite possibly, the smartest and hardest working human I knew. The question also revealed that what the world says about work often shapes our thinking more than what the Bible says about it, even from an early age.

The world frequently declares that a woman who invests herself fully in the work of home and children is wasting her potential and settling for an unfulfilling life of domestic drudgery and boredom. Often referred to as "just a mom," our culture seems to assume that stay-at-home mothers don't have a "real" vocation in which to find their identity. The Scriptures, on the other hand, command and commend the work of raising up the next generation in the home. From the beginning, God's plan for his world centered on fruitful multiplication. Remember that God blessed Adam and Eve and told them to reproduce and fill the world with more image-bearers (Gen. 1:28). The fulfillment of this mission cannot happen without women giving themselves to the difficult and vitally important work of bearing, feeding, and nurturing physical life. There is a clear Scriptural call for parents to intentionally bring up the next generation in the ways of the Lord (Deut. 6:4–9). There is also a clear command for older Christian women to teach younger believers what is good: "so train the young women to love their husbands and children, to be self-controlled, pure, working at home" (Tit. 2:4–5).

Let me be clear. While the Bible calls wives and mothers to be home-focused, there is no biblical prohibition on women working outside the home. In fact, the virtuous woman of Proverbs 31 is praised for pursuing work outside her home for the benefit of those within it (Prov. 31:16, 18, 24). There are numerous circumstances and seasons in which wives and mothers need to work outside the home for the benefit of their families. Furthermore, God, in his good providence, has not called all women to be wives and mothers of children in a nuclear family. The work of Christian women who don't have children is no less vitally important for God's kingdom purposes than the work of those who do. However, for the many God *has* called to be wives and mothers, nurturing life in the home is vitally important work. It should be a high priority to which we give ourselves whole-heartedly, as we serve the Lord through serving our families (Eph. 6:7). And this is work that should be highly esteemed by all, rather than viewed as insignificant and demeaning. Far from being menial, the work of home is a high calling that requires great strength and skill in a variety of areas. I'm encouraged by what G.K. Chesterton says about this:

> *"To be Queen Elizabeth within a definite area, deciding sales, banquets, labors and holidays; to be Whiteley within a certain area, providing toys, boots, sheets, cakes, and books, to be Aristotle within a certain area, teaching morals, manners, theology, and hygiene; I can understand how this might exhaust the mind, but I cannot imagine how it could narrow it. How can it be a large career to tell other people's children about the Rule of Three and a small career to tell one's own children about the universe? How can it be broad to be the same thing to everyone and narrow to be everything to someone? No, a woman's function is laborious, but because it is gigantic, not because it is minute."[3]*

Life-givers in the church

It was 9pm on a Tuesday night, and the modest-sized living room was lined wall-to-wall with college freshman girls. With students sitting on the furniture, the floor, and the stairs leading to another part of the house, the room was truly packed tight. Toma Knight, the college pastor's wife, had invited us to participate in a verse-by-verse Bible study through the book of James. That night was my first time in the Knight's home, but it wouldn't be my last. I quickly grew to love and respect Toma immensely. Love for Christ and passion for his Word simply oozed out of her. She usually couldn't talk about the Lord without tears of gratitude welling up. Toma mentored me during my college years—my first years living away from home. Throughout her life, she has welcomed untold numbers of college students from the church into her home to feed them, love them, and teach them the Scriptures. She loves others so genuinely, longing to help them grow in their devotion to Christ. Toma is the epitome of a spiritual mother.

The Bible calls women to be life-givers, not only in the home, but also in the church. Before the resurrected Jesus ascended into heaven, he gave his first followers a new work-mandate that built upon and expanded the original one given to Adam and Eve in Genesis 1. Jesus commanded his disciples to be fruitful and multiply by making more disciples (Matt. 28:19–20). In essence, he called all who identify with him by faith to the work of building and nurturing life in a new family—his church. This is done through evangelism (sharing the gospel and calling the lost to believe) and discipleship (helping believers grow in obedience to Christ). As we've seen, the church is a crucial part of God's mission to renew this sin-cursed world and fill it with his glory.

It's easy to leave the work of the church to pastors, leaders, missionaries, and those with a special call to vocational Christian ministry. *After all, that's what most of them are paid to do,* we think. This is a common assumption, but the Bible is clear that *all* believers have been spiritually gifted and called to the good work of building up Christ's body. Paul writes:

> *"And [Jesus] gave the apostles, the prophets, the evangelists,*
> *the shepherds and teachers, to equip the saints for the work*
> *of the ministry, for building up the body of Christ, until we*
> *all attain to the unity of the faith and of the knowledge of*
> *the Son of God, to mature manhood, to the measure of the*
> *stature of the fullness of Christ" (Eph. 4:11–13).*

When Jesus ascended to heaven post-resurrection, he gave a variety of spiritual gifts to his people, enabling us to fulfill the mission he gave us to do. Church leaders, particularly those who minister the Word of God, have been gifted to teach and equip *all* believers for the work of ministry, so the church will grow properly and eventually reach full maturity in Christ upon his return (Eph. 4:12–13). Regardless of whether a Christian woman is called to raise up physical children in the home, she is definitively called to help raise up spiritual children in the church. God's family isn't comprised of those who share blood but of those who share the same faith and Spirit; therefore, there are no childless women in the family of God. As women in Christ, we are *all* spiritual daughters and mothers, and this is lived out in a variety of ways as we use the different gifts God has bestowed on us to help his body grow.

Nurturing life in the church may look like regularly meeting a younger woman for coffee to study the Scriptures together. It could be opening your home weekly to host a small group, caring for children in the church nursery, or serving coffee and greeting people on Sunday mornings. It may look like preparing meals for those who are suffering, praying for and encouraging the fainthearted, or helping meet the financial needs of those struggling in your local fellowship. Some might play an instrument during the worship service on Sunday morning or make PowerPoint slides with song lyrics for the congregation. Others might teach in student ministry, write a letter of encouragement to an older believer, lead a women's Bible study or keep the church's website up to date.

As we seek to discern and use our gifts to serve the church, let's be careful not to create (or reinforce) that false sacred/secular dichotomy in our minds. We must remember that the work of nurturing life in the church is not disconnected from the work we do each ordinary day of the week. In fact, the work of the Great Commission in Matthew 28:19–20 begins wherever we are. Whether we labor in our homes, an office, a store, a classroom, a hospital, or anywhere else, the glorious task of making disciples begins there as we share the gospel with the lost and plead with them to turn to Christ. But our work doesn't end there. It culminates with serving the local church, faithfully using our gifts to cultivate spiritual life in others while trusting God to bring the growth.

Summing it up

As a psychology major at a public university, I put off taking a (supposedly difficult) research methods class until I was close to graduating. The class ended up not being as bad as expected, and I did well. After our final project, the professor asked about my future plans. Assuming I would pursue a Master's degree in some area of psychology, he wanted me to consider working for him as a research assistant. When I told him I was planning to get married following graduation and attend seminary with my husband to prepare for Christian ministry, he was surprised and puzzled. The expression on his face seemed to say, "Why in the world would you waste your potential on *that?*"

The world cannot understand the true purpose and value of all human work because the world is spiritually blind, dead in sin, and unable to glorify God. As those in Christ, we have been given new hearts and eyes to see. We now view our work through a gospel-shaped lens. We understand that laboring by faith in Christ for the glory of God and the good of those around us makes our work eternally significant.

Many of the good works God has prepared for us to do will not build a big bank account or garner a huge Instagram following, but in God's economy, work that is unseen and unsung by our culture can, ironically, be the most world-changing. Work that insists we die to the pursuit of our own names and pour ourselves out in service to others for the sake of *God's* name is revolutionary and eternal. As women rooted in Christ, let's faithfully tend the gardens he has assigned to our care. May we trust him to establish the work of our hands, causing it to bear fruit for his purposes and glory (Ps. 90:17).

Questions for reflection and discussion

1. When it comes to your work, are you more likely to feel pride or insecurity? Or do you swing between the two?

2. Read Genesis 1:28. What was the intended purpose of human work? How did humanity's relationship with work become distorted?

3. Read Ephesians 2:8–10. How is this passage both a humbling jolt and very good news for those who idolize self and work?

4. In thinking about the work you do (or want to do), how are you prone to draw sacred/secular divisions? How does

Ephesians 6:5–9 apply to both Christian employees and employers?

5. Contrast the world's view of women who pour themselves fully into the work of home and family with the Scripture's call for women to be life-givers in the home (see Titus 2:3–5). Have you been shaped more by the world or the Word in this area?

6. Read Ephesians 4:11–16. How are you using your gifts to nurture life in the church? If you're not, how can you begin?

7. Think of one practical way you can encourage another Christian woman whose work is different from yours. Rather than comparing, how can you spur her on to serve others and glorify God through her labors?

7

Authentic Friendship

Bearing with one another in love

*Walk in a manner worthy of the calling to which you have
been called, with all humility and gentleness, with patience,
bearing with one another in love, eager to maintain the unity
of the Spirit in the bond of peace.*
—*Ephesians 4:1–3*

It was a cold night in early spring 2009. I parked my car and
hustled into the large building, anxious to locate the warm
classroom quickly. I arrived to find the room quiet and mostly
empty. Only a few other women were in their seats. Not knowing
a soul, I chose a spot by myself toward the back. As more ladies
arrived, chatter filled the quiet room. Not naturally one to
initiate conversation with people I don't know, I busied myself
looking at my phone until a chipper voice beside me caught my
attention: "Hi! I'm Christy. What's your name?" A petite blonde
plopped down in the seat next to me with a friendly smile.

It was the first night of Seminary Wives Institute, intended
to help us prepare for vocational ministry with our husbands.

Adam and I had just moved over 500 miles from home to study at The Southern Baptist Theological Seminary. Adam had recently begun classes, and, although I planned to eventually earn a degree myself, we were attempting to find jobs and get our feet on the ground in a new city. The Seminary Wives Institute, a free program one night a week, seemed like a good place for me to start. I soon found that Christy had made the same decision.

The two of us began to chat and immediately realized we had a lot in common. Christy and her husband were also young newlyweds from the south who had just finished college and moved to attend seminary. Like us, they lived in a tiny apartment and were working retail jobs to make ends meet while pursuing Master's degrees. That first night in class, Christy and I exchanged phone numbers and made plans to get together for lunch and then for dinner with our husbands. The rest is history. We became fast friends and enjoyed a sweet friendship over the next four years of living in the same city.

Looking back, this was a fairly typical beginning to all my female friendships in the first two and a half decades of my life. From grade school through seminary, friendships came easily for me. This isn't because I'm especially likable or a fantastic friend to others. I think it has more to do with God's kindness and my circumstances. I was born and raised in an adorable small town, and I naturally clicked with some of the girls I grew up with. We were similar in every way—from our parents' socioeconomic status, to our religious upbringing, to our interests, aptitudes, and even clothing styles. These girls were precious gifts to me in my growing up years. In college, the same was true. Of course, none of the friendships I've mentioned were perfect (because no friendship is). There was disagreement and conflict here and there, but nothing major. Because friendship seemed relatively effortless, it was many years before I truly evaluated the kind of friend I am or thought deeply about how to develop and maintain Christian friendships.

Necessary, good, and hard

After our seminary years, friendships began to take a different shape for me. Adam was hired as the discipleship pastor at a mid-sized church in a smallish Alabama town. I was a stay-at-home mom with our second son on the way. We immediately met wonderful people in our new church—people who loved and cared for us so well. However, as I settled into long days at home caring for my little guy, I began to experience an emotion that was wholly foreign to me: loneliness. For twenty-five years, I had always had friends in the exact same season of life as me and ample time to spend with them. In our new church, most of the moms my age worked outside the home. There wasn't really anyone to call for a midweek play-date or a meet-up at the park. I didn't instantly connect with someone just like me. In fact, in those early months I felt a bit like an outsider in a community where everyone already had friends and extended family nearby. Periods of loneliness aren't fun, but it's often in the times of struggle and lack that God does the most beautiful work of transformation in our hearts. God used that time as a springboard to reshape my view of friendship. He began to help me understand it through the lens of the gospel.

Friendship is one of God's greatest gifts and one of life's highest blessings. Because we are made in the image of a relational God—a God who exists in the perfect fellowship of three persons—the desire for friendship is woven into the fabric of our DNA. We crave connection and companionship, longing to know and be known by others. We want to be in relationship with those who share our interests and those we can depend on in times of need. Friendships are important for healthy human flourishing. The great pastor and theologian Jonathan Edwards touched on this when he wrote, "The well-being and happiness of society is friendship. 'Tis the highest happiness of all moral agents."[1] Almost everything is better when shared with a friend.

Whether young or old, male or female, single or married, everyone needs and wants true friends. But friendships between sinners can be complex and challenging, and there are some specific problems that tend to rear their ugly heads in female friendships. Even in childhood, conflict, exclusivity, and cliquishness often exist among groups of girls, exposing insecurity among other problems. Friendships can become possessive or codependent, revealing our tendency to seek from people for what only God can give. Sadly, these problems don't necessarily improve with time and age, but difficulties of busyness, changing seasons, and changing locations all get added in. Friends grow up, get married, and move away. Once-close friendships fade and sometimes dissolve altogether. Every woman has probably experienced periods of loneliness in life—seasons when she couldn't seem to find a true friend. Then, there's the problem of trust and being authentic in friendship. Because of past wounds and fear of what others will think, it can be difficult to open ourselves up and be transparent.

Wonderfully, the gospel speaks into this messy business of friendship. For those who are *in Christ*, the good news of his life, death, and resurrection can redeem the broken parts of our friendships and reshape them in beautiful ways.

A true friend, a forever family

Foundationally, the gospel shapes our friendships by securing us a faithful friend who can never be lost. Although the words may sound trite and cheesy, the reality is deeply comforting: If you are in Christ, Jesus is your true and forever friend. In a world where friendships (even among believers) are full of challenges and changes, this truth offers us profound peace and security.

Jesus is the only friend who chose you, loved you, died for you, and pursued a relationship with you when you were totally unlovable. No other friend could ever love you with that depth of affection, devotion, and sacrifice (Jn. 15:13). In Christ, God has given you a friend who knows everything about you and will never hurt you, despite how you treat him on any given day. Jesus is a constant companion in your life both now and for all eternity, regardless of how your other friendships ebb, flow, and change over the course of time. He is a friend who not only knows *you* but also wants you to know *him*, and he is the only one who can meet your deepest, most fundamental relational needs. An intimate friendship with Christ is the foundation for fulfilling, God-glorifying friendships on earth.

But Jesus is a friend I can't see! My eleven-year-old recently articulated what many of us are probably thinking. Jesus is a friend we can't see, hear, or touch in a physical sense right now, and as embodied creatures we naturally long for physical presence. I reminded my son that God, in his kindness, has not only given us Christ, but he has also given us his body—the church. While Christ alone is the fountainhead able to satisfy our deepest relational thirst (Jn. 4:14), he cares for our relational needs in many ways through the members of his body. The church is made up of those we can share tangible friendship with right now.

Earlier in chapter four, we saw that God has united all who are *in Christ* in one body called the church (Eph. 2:18–19). Paul reiterates the depth of the church's unity in Ephesians 4, when he writes:

> *"There is one body and one Spirit—just as you were called to the one hope that belongs to your call—one Lord, one faith, one baptism, one God and Father of all who is over all and through all and in all" (Eph. 4:4–6).*

Believers around the world and down through time have all been spiritually baptized into the body of Christ and share the same faith, Spirit, Lord, and Father. This profound spiritual unity is to be lived out practically within local churches as Christians participate in deep, intimate friendships—friends bound by Christ and committed to one another as eternal family members.

We tend to think of friends and family as separate relational entities, but, according to the Scriptures, the very best friends are those who are as loyal as a biological sibling should be: "A man of many companions may come to ruin, but there is a friend who sticks closer than a brother" (Prov. 18:24). In his book *When the Church Was a Family*, professor Joe Hellerman explains the significance of sibling relationships in the ancient world:

> *"...loyalty to one's siblings was at the center of ancient Mediterranean sensibilities... the most intense emotional bonding did not occur between spouses in marriage but between siblings who shared the same father... If there was one place in the ancient world where a person could expect*

> *to encounter a united front, it was in the descent-group*
> *family of blood brothers and sisters."*[2]

In the ancient biblical world, biological siblings were the most faithful friends. Siblings were the ones who knew and loved each other best—the ones who had each other's backs. It makes sense, then, that Paul so frequently used the family metaphor and the language of "brothers and sisters" (139 times in his thirteen New Testament letters) rather than the language of "friends" when addressing relationships in the church. Hellerman explains, "Like Jesus [Matt 12:46–50], Paul viewed the church as a surrogate family... For Paul, sibling unity in the Christian church is a logical extension of his understanding of the world in which he lived."[3]

Who are your people?

You've probably heard someone say "Those are my people!" Whether it's a reference to family members, friends, a sports team, or a political party, to consider any group "your people" is to strongly identify yourself with them. Your people are those with whom you feel you most belong, whether it's because of blood relations, common interests, a shared worldview, and/or mutual love and affection. In some cases, you might say your people are those you know and love best... and those who know and love you best in return.

In the second half of Ephesians, Paul explains how the profound spiritual unity of the universal church is to be lived out visibly in the local church. In order to apply this instruction rightly to our own lives today, we need to understand two assumptions Paul makes. First, Paul takes for granted that to be in Christ is to be an active member of a local church. Second, he assumes that Christians see the church as *their people*—the group with whom they most strongly identify—because of the spiritual unity which transcends all other similarities and differences. Practically, this means that the believer's deepest friendships—those who live as "friends-like-family"—will form within the local church.

Now, please hear me out. The Scriptures nowhere indicate that believers shouldn't enjoy rich friendships with people outside of their own local church. Neither do they assume we will share a close friendship with every single member in our church (or that our friendships will never change or fade). Because of our human limitations, these are impossibilities. The Scriptures do, however, teach that being united to Christ by faith means his people become our people in a way that is more than just theoretical. We desperately need authentic, sibling-like friendships in the family of God—friends we can eat, laugh, and pray with... friends we can lean on for help when crisis hits. We were not created to walk through this life alone.

Throughout the New Testament there are approximately fifty-nine "one another" commands, instructing the church on how to practically live in relationship. In Ephesians alone we are called to bear with one another in love (Eph. 4:2), speak truth to one another (Eph. 4:25), be kind to one another (Eph. 4:32), forgive one another (Eph. 4:32), sing psalms and hymns with one another (Eph. 5:19), and submit to one another (Eph. 5:21). Elsewhere we are told to outdo one another in showing honor (Rom. 12:10), have concern for one another (1 Cor. 12:25), serve one another (Gal. 5:13), and the list goes on and on. We cannot obey these commands if the only time we're with God's people is a couple of hours on Sunday mornings. The fulfillment of these commands requires additional time together—grabbing a coffee before work, opening our homes, serving side by side—and a counter-cultural commitment to God's people as our people. As we faithfully live out the spiritual unity of God's family in tangible ways, deep relational bonds form—sometimes between otherwise unlikely friends.

Unlikely friendships

When it comes to friendship, most of us have one or two natural proclivities that affect our relationships in the church. The first tendency is to sit back and wait for others to approach us, hoping they will see us and meet our relational needs. The second tendency is to do the approaching, but move only toward those with whom we share obvious similarities. As the gospel reorients our understanding of friendship, the Holy Spirit empowers us to live in ways that override these natural propensities.

The many "one another" commands in Scripture call us to be proactive and generous in relationships by making the first move toward others. Not once does the Bible hint that we should sit back and wait for someone to "one another" us first. But as we pursue others, we must be careful not to show partiality (Jas. 2:1), reaching out only to those who dress like us, think like us, or happen to be in the same season of life. Let's be mindful not to only reach out to those who are outwardly put together, or those we find it easy to talk to. We cannot be relationally close with every single person in our church (and we will naturally gravitate toward those with similarities), but the Spirit empowers us to show love indiscriminately.

During the season of loneliness I experienced at our first church, the Lord proved so kind. As Adam and I poured ourselves into the life of the church, he blessed us with some of the sweetest, unexpected friendships. I never found a young mom friend to have regular playdates with, but I did have two precious middle-aged couples who loved my children like their own grandchildren. These couples babysat for us, opened their homes to us, and just really loved us well. I also bonded with a younger sister in Christ—a recent college graduate eager to grow in her faith. Early on, she reached out to me for discipleship, and we quickly developed a friendship built on our shared love for Christ as well as our mutual love for reading, studying theology, and running. Some other precious friendships were formed with a group of women of varying ages, all who desired to grow spiritually and serve in women's ministry. We regularly studied, learned, prayed, planned, and led together. Had I found people just like me, I might have missed out on these dear friendships in the Lord.

In our current church, the Lord has given me a variety of friendships, and I've experienced the full gamut of emotions in these relationships. I've felt the gratitude of having sisters in Christ immediately welcome me into their lives when I was new at church. I've enjoyed friendships with single women in different seasons of life. I've known the heartache of friends moving away and the excitement of blossoming fellowship with new friends. I've cherished the relational closeness of "friends-like-family" and the gift of sisters I can pray and share my heart with. I've also experienced seasons of loneliness, as well as conflict and hurt in friendship. These experiences reveal both the beauty and challenges of relationships within the church. Because we are recovering sinners, maintaining harmony is hard work. It requires the power of the Spirit and our own grace-driven effort to practically live out the unity we share in Christ.

You're unified, so maintain unity

The typical problems that crop up in female friendships such as cliquishness, exclusivity, codependency, jealousy, and fear of man sadly infect relationships among sisters in Christ as well. These are major hindrances to the Christian unity Paul commands believers to safeguard when he writes:

> "...walk in a manner worthy of the calling to which you have been called with all humility and gentleness, with patience, bearing with one another in love, eager to maintain the unity of the Spirit in the bond of peace" (Eph. 4:1–3).

In this text, Paul outlines the heart posture necessary for healthy friendships to flourish within the church. We must be humble, gentle, patient, and willing to lovingly persevere with one another. Let's break these down.

Being humble

In his book *The Freedom of Self-Forgetfulness*, Tim Keller writes, "the essence of gospel humility is not thinking more of myself or less of myself, it is thinking of myself less."[4] In other words, humble people are primarily focused on Jesus and others. When it comes to cultivating and maintaining friendships, humble women concentrate on *being* a true friend to others. Humility enables us to approach those in our church with a

"There you are! How can I love you?" attitude, rather than a "Here I am! I demand that you meet my needs!" one. True humility enables us to make the first move. It enables us to sit beside the person who is alone during worship, initiate a coffee date with a woman we don't know very well, open our home to others even if the invites don't get returned as often, or ask a newcomer along to a gathering of familiar friends. Humility prompts us to pray for our sisters regularly, thinking about their needs and not just our own. Humility motivates us to *be* the friend we wish we had.

Where pride says, "I can handle things on my own," humility acknowledges the truth that we need help, and that God intends for his people to live interconnected lives of service to one another. When faced with physical, spiritual, and emotional needs, humble women are vulnerable enough to ask for and receive help from trusted sisters (and brothers) in Christ. In addition, humble women recognize their need for friendship with multiple people in the church because no one person can meet every need. Humility equips us to move toward our sisters in Christ with authenticity—to ask an older woman to disciple us, confess sin to a friend, request prayer, solicit a ride to the airport or help watching the kids, to plead with a sister to remind us of the truth when we desperately need to hear it, to share our trials and joys.

Being gentle and patient

Because we are not yet perfected, it will be necessary to endure patiently with one another through the pangs of sin and suffering. In friendships within the body, we are going to regularly bump into one another's sin patterns and sometimes get hurt. To be gentle and patient in friendship means that we strive to treat others the way Christ treats us. We aren't harshly critical of another's shortcomings, and we don't automatically write off the relationship when things get heavy and difficult. Patiently bearing with others means we trust God is transforming our friends (and us) into the image of Christ in *his* timing rather than ours. We will need to endure patiently with one another in love, seeking and extending forgiveness often (Eph. 4:32) as we suffer and battle remaining sin on the road to glory.

Love speaks truth

Does gently and patiently bearing with one another in love mean we turn a blind eye to the sins of our sisters in Christ? In the name of unity, it can be extremely tempting to sweep things under the rug, avoiding difficult conversations that could potentially lead to conflict. The Bible teaches that true love is not easily angered (1 Cor. 13:5) and covers a multitude of petty offenses (1 Pet. 4:8), but it also teaches us to lovingly speak truth to our sisters in the Lord. There are times when we must speak a hard word about sin to help one another grow up in Christ. Paul writes:

> *"...speaking the truth in love, we are to grow up in every way into him who is the head, into Christ... having put away falsehood, let each one of you speak the truth with his neighbor, for we are members of one another" (Eph. 4:15, 25).*

Because we belong to one another, our greatest desire for our sisters should be to see them grow in Christ-likeness. If we become aware of sin that is stunting their spiritual growth and hindering true unity in the body, we must lovingly bring that to their attention and implore them to repent (Matt. 18:15). Likewise, if a friend sees sin in our life and confronts us in love, we must self-evaluate and repent with requisite humility. This means there will be some hard and awkward conversations in authentic friendships—words spoken in love that will still sting. Regardless of which end of the conversation we are on (and we should be on both at times), may we learn to see these difficult interactions for what they are: means of God's grace in keeping us from the path of destruction. As the proverb says, "Faithful are the wounds of a friend" (Prov. 27:6).

Let's be careful, though, not to speak only the truth about sin. When our sin is exposed, we desperately need good news and hope! We need help remembering the full forgiveness and promised transformation that are ours in Christ. As we lovingly tell the truth in friendship—the truth about both sin *and* its gospel remedy—we're helping one another put off vices like bitterness, wrath, anger, clamor, and malice (Eph. 4:31) and put on kindness, tender-hearts, and forgiveness instead (Eph. 4:32).

Summing it up

Looking back, I can truly say I'm thankful friendship hasn't always come easily as an adult because God has used the challenges to do necessary work in me. Most importantly, he has driven me to greater dependence on Jesus as my ultimate true friend. He's also exposed my sin in friendship and is slowly transforming me into a more Christ-like friend to others.

How is it possible to survive the seasons of loneliness we are all sure to have—those periods when we don't feel deeply connected with anyone in our church, and no one seems willing or able to meet our friendship needs? In addition, how do we become humble, patient, and kind friends to others both in times of loneliness and times of relational flourishing? The only answer is Jesus Christ.

Deep, sibling-like friendships within the church only work well when each member has a strong friendship with the Head. When we really believe Jesus is the source of all we need, we learn to continually abide (Jn. 15) and trust him in our earthly relationships. This means we turn to Jesus in times of loneliness, pleading with him to meet our needs and believing by faith that this pain is not forever (Rev. 21:3–4). It means we have the confidence to move toward others in love, even when we don't yet have the assurance that we will be loved well in return. It means that, by Christ's power, we can grow in humility, learn to be vulnerable, confess sin, and seek or grant forgiveness often. Finally, it means that we can deeply enjoy our friends without expecting them to be for us what only Christ can be—a constant companion and sure source of security and joy. What a friend we have in Jesus! As gospel-shaped women, may we live like it's true, and may we enjoy the richest earthly friendships as a result.

Questions for reflection and discussion

1. Think back over your friendships throughout the course of life. What have been some of your greatest challenges and greatest joys? What about your friendships currently?
2. Why can friendships be so complex and difficult?
3. Read John 15:13–16 and Ephesians 4:4–6. What does the gospel secure for us in terms of friendship? How does this bring you comfort?
4. If someone were to ask, "Who are your people?" what would you say? Which attitude mentioned in Ephesians

4:1–3 feels most challenging as you cultivate friendships within your church?

5. Do you tend to sit back and wait for others to pursue you in friendship? When you do pursue others, are you likely to move toward only those who are like you? Think of one way you can reach out to a sister who is different from you (different age, season, etc.) this week.

6. Read Ephesians 4:15 & 25. Do you have sisters in Christ who know you well enough to call out your sin and remind you of the hope of the gospel? Do you have sisters for whom you can do the same? What are some practical ways you can cultivate "friends-like-family" relationships in your local church?

7. To grow in being a Christ-like friend to others, we must develop a deeper friendship with Christ. What are some practical ways to do this?

8

Temples Not Idols

Glorifying God in our physical bodies

In him you also are being built together into a dwelling place
for God by the Spirit.
—Ephesians 2:22

But sexual immorality and all impurity or covetousness must
not even be named among you, as is proper among saints…
For you may be sure of this, that everyone who is sexually
immoral or impure, or who is covetous (that is, an idolater),
has no inheritance in the kingdom of Christ and God.
—Ephesians 5:3, 5

I remember when I first became insecure about my body. I was fifteen years old and needed new jeans. Seemingly overnight, the size zero pants of my rail-thin middle-school years ceased to fit, and I had to buy bigger clothing. It's clear to me now that I was filling out naturally and developing the soft curves of womanhood, but at the time I wholeheartedly believed I was losing control and getting fat. Prone to struggle with self-focused perfectionism, I had at some point internalized the lie that to be beautiful is to be thin… very thin.

During my sophomore year of high school, the obsession with my weight became so consuming that I developed an eating disorder. Any weight gain was unacceptable to me. If the numbers on the scale went up or my clothing felt even the slightest bit snug, I freaked out. Having total control over the size of my body became so important to me that I restricted my caloric intake to a dangerous low while exercising excessively. I remember sitting at the school lunch table, thinking through which parts of lunch I would allow myself to eat and how I would try to burn those calories later in the day. It wasn't uncommon for me to eat only half of a small chicken sandwich at the midday meal and then attempt to run three to six miles after school.

My sense of self-worth was totally wrapped up in having a thin body, and I worshiped at the altar of my ideal-sized figure. Although I loved the Lord and knew this was an area of my life not surrendered to him, I resisted relinquishing control, even to the point of lying and trying to hide my problem from my parents and friends. I loved and longed for a worldly conception of physical beauty far too much to want to crush my idol. Sadly, I didn't realize just how close my idol came to crushing me.

Love/hate relationship

As women, we have a complicated relationship with our bodies, don't we? We can both revere ourselves, being hyper-focused on how we look and feel, and at the same time disdain the body we've been given for failing to meet cultural standards of beauty. We look in the mirror hoping to find an object worthy of our worship and are sometimes disappointed or even ashamed of what we see. As lovers of beauty, we naturally long to display beauty through our bodies, and this desire isn't necessarily bad. The problem comes when our conceptions of beauty are formed more by magazines, television, and Instagram than by God's Word, and our motivation to be beautiful is self- rather than God-focused.

Those who've been in church for a while are probably aware that the Bible emphasizes the importance of cultivating inner beauty above outer beauty. We've heard passages like Proverbs 31:30: "Charm is deceitful, and beauty is vain, but a woman who fears the Lord is to be praised." We might remember the Apostle Peter's exhortation to women: "Do not let your adorning be external—the braiding of hair and the putting on of gold jewelry, or the clothing you wear—but let your adorning be the hidden person of the heart" (1 Pet. 3:3–4).

These passages reveal that, while humans tend to focus on what we can see, God is primarily concerned with the inner person, which cannot be seen (1 Sam. 16:7). While this important theme runs throughout the Bible, it doesn't mean the physical body is insignificant or that God is unconcerned about what his creatures do with their bodies. Quite the contrary! If passages such as Proverbs 31:30 and 1 Peter 3:3–4 are the only parts of Scripture shaping how we understand and treat our physical selves, our theology of the body will be quite lopsided. Applied in isolation, these verses could lead us to believe the body is irrelevant to our spiritual health—but that still wouldn't keep us from desiring flawless skin, toned thighs, and a flat stomach. As Christian women, we need more than a few exhortations about focusing on inner beauty. As important as this is, we need a robust theology of the body, derived from the whole of Scripture. It's crucial for us to see how the gospel is good news for our bodies as well as our souls.

Spirit good, body bad?

Have you ever heard someone say, "This body's just a shell; the real me is inside"? This sounds super spiritual at first blush, but it's actually reminiscent of an ancient heresy called Gnosticism that infiltrated the early church. The Gnostics "disparaged the material world as the realm of death, decay, and destruction [believing it to be] the source of evil."[1] In other words, they believed the human spirit was intrinsically good and the body was intrinsically bad. Gnosticism made a sharp division between the body and the person,[2] claiming that the soul (which was thought to be the true person) needed to be liberated from the body and the entire physical realm. This understanding of the body is fundamentally at odds with the Christian worldview.

The opening chapters of Genesis reveal that God created gender-specific, embodied human beings and declared them "very good" (Gen. 1:31). Christianity has an undeniably high view of the human body. According to the Scriptures, our bodies are not accidental or incidental; they are intentionally made by God with a purpose. Each person is a union of body and soul, carefully woven together by the Creator. When King David considered the intricacy of his personhood, he worshiped the God who formed both his soul and body: "I praise you, for I am fearfully and wonderfully made" (Ps. 139:14). Regardless of how we feel about the size, shape, and look of our own body, each of us has the physical flesh God designed for us. Our bodies are intrinsically good because they were made by a good God who declared them to be so.

C.S. Lewis writes:

> "Christianity is almost the only one of the great religions which thoroughly approves of the body—which believes that matter is good, that God Himself once took on a human body, that some kind of body is going to be given to us in Heaven and is going to be an essential part of our happiness, our beauty and our energy."[3]

The human body is a beautiful and necessary part of God's plan for his creatures, but it was never meant to be worshiped. Human bodies make very bad gods because they cannot save us.

Bodies broken by sin

When my second son was six years old, he woke up one day complaining of a sharp pain in his chest. The pain continued to increase without relief until we eventually took him to the emergency room. Doctors ran tests to diagnose the problem. They knew something was wrong, but it took multiple tests and more than two days in the hospital for them to figure out what the problem was. We don't have to live long in the world to know something is wrong with our bodies. They feel pain, get sick, and don't always work the way they should. They're hard to satisfy, cause us insecurity and shame, and ultimately? They die. It's clear our bodies are broken, but because the effects of this brokenness are myriad, we easily misdiagnose the root cause.

The Gnostics misdiagnosed the source of the problem by conflating creation and the fall. They believed the human soul "fell" from the spiritual realm into the physical realm and was corrupted by taking on a body during creation.[4] This is far from what the Bible teaches. Genesis tells us the entire physical realm, including human bodies, was created good, and it was sin's entrance into the world that left no part of creation uncorrupted (Rom. 8:20–22). Every part of our humanity, both body and soul, has been affected by sin.

In this fallen world, our bodies are not only cursed with frailty, disability, disease, and death, but they have also become objects and agents of the idolatry flowing from our hearts. Although our bodies were created to be used for God's purposes and glory, in our sin we all live with a "my body, my choice" mentality. We believe the lie that our bodies are ultimately for *us*, and, therefore, we're free to do whatever we want with them. This belief typically plays out in one of two ways. Either we seek to control our bodies for our own glory, or we are controlled *by* our bodily appetites for our own pleasure. Seeking to control our bodies may look like hyper-fitness obsession, self-starvation, or selfies posted online. Being controlled by our bodies often manifests as laziness, overeating, substance abuse, or sexual immorality. When we give in to every appetite, we function as if what we eat, drink, or do sexually really doesn't matter; it's just body stuff—physical cravings needing to be appeased. These are two different sides of body idolatry, but in both cases, humans are worshiping and serving the creature rather than the Creator (Rom. 1:25) and devaluing the human body in the process. This self-worship eventually results in feelings of deep shame.

Do you remember what happened when Adam and Eve rebelled against God? As soon as they ate the forbidden fruit, they became self-conscious of their nakedness (Gen. 3:7). After using their bodies to turn against the God who made them, they suddenly felt exposed, insecure, and ashamed. In fear, they attempted to cover their shame by covering their bodies. Because we are born with a sinful nature inherited from our first parents, we come into this world seemingly programmed to feel bodily insecurity.[5] And this vulnerability only grows as we continue to sin and are sinned against. When we're consumed with having a body the world says is worthy of worship, when we use our bodies to actively disobey God, or when our bodies are used by others for sinful purposes, we are left wanting to hide. Like our hearts, our bodies are deeply broken by sin and in need of redemption.

His body exposed for us

As a Christian, do you ever experience the frustration of wanting to obey God in your *heart*, yet feeling a strong pull toward sin in your *body*? You want to care less about your physical appearance, but your eyes are constantly drawn to the mirror and the intense scrutiny that results either in self-worship or self-loathing. You want to turn to the Lord when anxious, but in moments of heavy stress, a cookie binge or a little too much wine really hits the spot. You want to honor God through sexual purity, but you experience (and maybe act upon) strong temptations toward sexual fulfillment outside God's good boundary lines. In each case, you probably feel discouraged that sinning with your body still comes so naturally. You're not alone.

In Ephesians 5:3–5, Paul warns the church to avoid sexual immorality, impurity, and covetousness—behaviors which characterize unbelievers and incur God's judgment. He writes:

> *"...for because of these things the wrath of God comes upon the sons of disobedience. Therefore do not become partners with them; for at one time you were darkness, but now you are light in the Lord. Walk as children of light"* (Eph. 5:6–8).

To walk as children of light means believers "take no part in the unfruitful works of darkness but instead expose them" (Eph. 5:11). Instead of hiding in the dark shadows of our bodily transgressions, we flee these sins by allowing the light to reveal them for what they are. This exposure is initially painful (who likes to admit their sin?), so it's important to note that Paul doesn't offer this exhortation from a morally superior high horse. He writes as one who knows the struggle personally. In his letter to the Romans, Paul laments that he is still so prone to sin with his body while his mind simultaneously longs to please the Lord (Rom. 7:22–23). Frustrated, he cries out, "Wretched man that I am! Who will deliver me from this body of death? Thanks be to God through Jesus Christ our Lord!" (Rom. 7:24–25). Paul understood that Jesus brings salvation not only for his sinful soul, but also for his broken body.

As Jesus hung naked on the cross, dying a shameful, public death by crucifixion, he (quite literally) brought our evil deeds into the light. In bearing our sins in his own sinless body (1 Pet. 2:24), Jesus was exposed *for us*. In him, all our evil was laid bare in the glorious light of a holy God, and the agony of that exposure was incalculable. However, the pain of judgment soon gave way to the healing power of resurrection light. Paul writes, "But when anything is exposed by the light, it becomes visible, for anything that becomes visible is light. Therefore it says, 'Awake,

O sleeper, and arise from the dead, and Christ will shine on you'" (Eph. 5:13–14).

If you are in Christ, your sins were exposed and judged in *his* sacrificial death. And his resurrection shows that the victory over sin is decisive and complete. As a result, you no longer live in shame and darkness; you get to live as a child of light! While this doesn't mean you won't ever struggle with bodily sin (remember our salvation is past, present, and future), it does mean you don't need to cower and hide in the fear of being exposed. Because Jesus was exposed for you, you can bring your remaining sin into his gospel light through humble confession and repentance. You can trust him to forgive and progressively transform you as you await the full redemption of your body (Rom. 8:23). Our physicality still aches under the weight of sickness, pain, and remaining sin in this life, but one day we will be set free from them all! When Jesus returns, he will resurrect the dead and give perfect, sinless, bodies to all who are found in him (1 Cor. 6:14).

So, how does Christ transform the way we view and use our bodies in the meantime? And what hope and help does his gospel light bring to our physical selves right now?

A dwelling place for God

When I was a teenager in the throes of anorexia, I didn't want anyone to know about it because I didn't really want help. I kept my sin in the dark because I greatly feared losing control over my body and gaining weight as a result. By God's grace, and despite my attempted cover-ups, my parents discovered I had a problem. In their wisdom, they knew that the problem was spiritual as much as it was physical and psychological. They arranged for me to start seeing a counselor and a nutritionist, but they also spoke a lot of biblical truth to me themselves. Among other things, my parents taught me that my body is not my own to do with as I please. They continually reminded me that my body belongs to Christ… and that this is very good news!

The thought of our bodies being owned by another tends to make us bristle. This is partly because of our sinful desire for autonomy from God, but it's also because we've seen horrifying injustices occur when people believe they can own other people. Dehumanizing atrocities such as slavery, sex trafficking, and other forms of abuse are the result. To be the property of sinful humans is a travesty, but to be owned by a holy, loving God is humanity's only true hope. As the Heidelberg Catechism says, my "only comfort in life and death [is] that I am not my own, but belong with body and soul, both in life and death, to my faithful Savior Jesus Christ."[6] Author Sam Allberry sums it up succinctly: "The only way our bodies can be restored and redeemed by Jesus is through them belonging to Jesus."[7]

In Ephesians 2, we learned that those who are in Christ are not only inseparably joined to Jesus but are also spiritually joined to each other as members of God's household (Eph. 2:19). Paul goes on to explain that, incredibly, the members of the household comprise the house itself. Corporately, the people of God make up the new temple where God's very presence dwells. He writes, "In him you also are being built together into a dwelling place for God by the Spirit" (Eph. 2:22). Paul explains this glorious reality to the church in Corinth as he seeks to correct their wrong view of the body: "…do you not know that your body is a temple of the Holy Spirit within you, whom you have from God? You are not your own, for you were bought with a price. So glorify God in your body" (1 Cor. 6:19–20).

Christ purchased believers at the steep price of his own blood. We belong to him. Our bodies are not just random blobs of matter, disconnected from our inner selves and the "truly important" spiritual realities. No, our bodies are an essential part of us, and we belong wholly to the Lord for his purposes and glory. In Christ, our bodies are no longer ground zero for our own idolatrous purposes; rather, they are the dwelling place of his Holy Spirit and a vital tool for carrying out good works. This has two major implications: First, it matters significantly what we do (and don't do) with our bodies. Second, we have the Holy Spirit living within, and he enables us to resist bodily sin.

Not for immorality and idolatry

I want to look like her. We rarely say the words. Many times, we don't even consciously think them. However, the desire is often rooted so deeply within that we overlook the various ways it motivates us. Whether we recognize it or not, we've all internalized certain ideals of bodily beauty. These ideals are shaped, in large part, by looking at other women and believing they are the standard. Maybe it's the toned, suntanned woman on the cover of a magazine. Maybe it's the women we watch on sitcoms or see at the gym. Maybe it's muscular athletes, pencil-thin models, or women with feminine curves. Maybe it's the women that seem to always have the attention of men, or the girls posting the selfies that get thousands of likes on social media. Over the course of a lifetime, millions of images (and commentary on those images) work together to shape our ideals of what's beautiful and desirable. Body idolatry is often the result of attempting to achieve those ideals and have them validated in us by others. In other words, body idolatry flows from coveting what is not ours. Whether we want it for our own glory or our own pleasure, coveting the body of another image-bearer as a commodity is not the way of the Christian.

This is why Paul doesn't mince words when he writes:

> *"But sexual immorality and all impurity or covetousness must not even be named among you, as is proper among saints… For you may be sure of this, that everyone who is sexually immoral or impure, or who is covetous (that is, an idolater), has no inheritance in the kingdom of Christ and God" (Eph. 5:3, 5).*

As we touched on earlier, immorality and idolatry characterize unbelievers, but the bodies of believers are members of Christ (1 Cor. 6:15). Thus, we are not to present our "members to sin as instruments for unrighteousness" but rather present our "members to God as instruments for righteousness" (Rom. 6:13). The Holy Spirit enables us to recognize and turn away from the many ways we practice idolatry and immorality with our bodies. He helps us cultivate a new ideal of bodily beauty—God's ideal. The Scriptures teach that a beautiful body is one fully devoted to God and set apart for his service.

A living sacrifice

During high school, I coveted a thinner physique, so I sacrificed the health and wellness of my body to an idol through self-starvation. There are numerous ways we sacrifice our bodies to idols—when we binge eat or turn to substances to feel better, when we deny our bodies adequate sleep and exercise, when we dress our bodies in certain ways for attention, and when we go too far with someone we're not married to. In light of Christ's sacrifice, God commands us to turn away from idols and surrender our physical selves wholly to him. After expounding the glories of the gospel (for eleven whole chapters!), Paul writes the following words to the church in Rome: "I appeal to you therefore, brothers, by the mercies of God, to present your bodies as a living sacrifice, holy and acceptable to God, which is your spiritual worship" (Rom. 12:1).

What does it mean to be a living sacrifice? Think about what was required of the people of God under the old covenant. They regularly had to slay innocent animals and present them to God on the altar to make atonement for their sin. One can only imagine what a bloody, messy, and weighty process this must have been. Sacrificial death was required because of sin. As new covenant believers, our situation is different. Because Christ offered himself as the once-for-all atoning sacrifice for sinners, we no longer have to present offerings of sacrificial death to God. On the contrary, we get to give God the precious offering of a sacrificial *life*—one in which we devote our bodily energy and vitality completely to him.[8]

To offer the body to God as a living sacrifice means not only that we turn away from using it for our own sinful agendas, but that we also intentionally use it for God's kingdom purposes. When we use our mouths to speak truth (Eph. 4:25) and graciously build others up (Eph. 4:29), we are a living sacrifice. When our hands do honest work and generously share with those in need (Eph. 4:28), we are a living sacrifice. When our legs walk alongside others in selfless service and love (Eph. 5:2), we are a living sacrifice.

Our bodies belong to the Lord, and it is our job to steward them accordingly. A steward is a caretaker of the property of another, and we are to care for our bodies in ways that honor our Master and equip us for his service. The sad reality, however, is that we often blur the lines between faithful stewardship and sinful idolatry. We need biblical wisdom and the guidance of the Holy Spirit to help us care well for our bodies with the right motivation. Do the Scriptures speak to the practical aspects of bodily care—things like diet, exercise, and sleep?

The world teaches us to see physical fitness and healthy eating primarily as a means of looking and feeling good. Advertisements, personal trainers, and social media train us to think diet and exercise are ultimately about *us*. The Bible, on the other hand, shows us that faithful stewardship of the body is motivated by a desire to serve God and others. As new covenant believers, the Scriptures give us no diet requirements. Because all foods have been made clean by Christ (Mk. 7:14–19), there is Christian freedom when it comes to what we eat and drink (1 Tim. 4:4). However, our decisions about food and drink should be driven by a desire for God's glory (1 Cor. 10:31), and we must always be controlled by the Spirit rather than by what we put in our bodies: "And do not get drunk with wine, for that is debauchery, but be filled with the Spirit" (Eph. 5:18). The Bible doesn't outline how often we should work out, but it does command us to put physical fitness in its proper place on the priority list: "for while bodily training is of some value, godliness is of value in every way, as it holds promise for the present life and also for the life to come" (1 Tim. 4:8).

Does this give us permission to eat whatever we want and be a bunch of couch potatoes? Of course not! As those walking by the Spirit, we must practice self-control (Gal. 5:23) rather than being mastered by our appetites (1 Cor. 6:12–13). Healthy eating and regular exercise are valuable for strengthening us to expend our bodies in service to Christ and others during our years on earth. In this sense, good stewardship of our individual, physical bodies actually strengthens the body of Christ by keeping each part working properly (Eph. 4:16). This means sometimes we should hit the gym when we would rather succumb to laziness, and other times we should skip the gym because our time and energy are needed in service to others. The Spirit helps us discern what faithful stewardship looks like each day and in each season.

Summing it up

The body idolatry and resulting eating disorder of my teenage years were not resolved overnight. Repentance and change were progressive but, by God's grace, they did happen (and are still happening). As the good news of the gospel got deeper into my bones with each passing year, the Holy Spirit changed my desires and motivations. He enabled me to care for my body as a temple rather than control it as an idol, but that process of change was gradual—like slowly prying open a tightly clenched fist, finger by finger.

Although I started eating adequately years before, it wasn't until I had children that I really saw how the beauty of my body involved so much more than looking a certain way. As I learned to lay down my time, my avid running, my figure, and my sleep to birth and care for children, I understood in a fresh way what good news the gospel is for my physicality. Through Jesus' sacrifice, I am forgiven of all the ways I have worshiped and misused my body. By his Spirit's power, I can shift my focus from loving, loathing, or trying to sculpt what I see in the mirror and instead steward my body for sacrificial service to Christ. Although my mortal flesh will continue to age and weaken as it creeps toward death, I have the sure hope that my body will one day be resurrected to immortality. If you are in Christ, you have that same hope. A day is coming when we will receive bodies that never face sickness, suffering, or sin again. Thanks be to God!

Questions for reflection and discussion

1. In what ways can women have a love/hate relationship with their bodies? What does this look like in your life?

2. Why do we often fall into the trap of thinking that the body is bad? How does Genesis 1:31 and Psalm 139:14 correct this view?

3. Is your tendency to control your body for your own glory, to be controlled by your bodily appetites for your own pleasure, or both? How does this show itself in your life?

4. Read Ephesians 2:22, 5:2 and 5:8–14. How is Jesus' sacrificial death and resurrection good news for our bodies as well as our souls?

5. Read 1 Corinthians 6:19–20. Do you bristle when you read that your body belongs to God? Why? Explain why this is really a comforting reality.

6. What does it mean to be a living sacrifice? How can we use our bodies for good?

7. How does the call to offer your body as a living sacrifice to God shape your views (and practice) of diet and exercise? Are you in a season when you need to eat and exercise more, less, or differently in order to better glorify God in your body?

9

Sexuality and Marriage

A picture not an end

*"Therefore a man shall leave his father and mother and
hold fast to his wife, and the two shall become one flesh."
This mystery is profound, and I am saying that it refers
to Christ and the church.*
—Ephesians 5:31–32

$\mathcal{I}$ met my future husband just a few months after my sixteenth birthday. "You and Adam would be perfect for each other!" a mutual friend declared with absolute confidence before introducing us. I rolled my eyes and thought, *Yeah, right!* I had recently (and somewhat rashly) determined that none of the boys in our area were "marriage material," so there was no point in dating until I went off to college. Enter Adam Rice. We met in December 2002, not long after the Holy Spirit awakened him to genuine faith in Christ. Adam was a senior in high school, hungering to know the Lord deeply and longing to get to know friends who shared his faith.

After we met, it didn't take Adam long to pursue a relationship with me, but I stubbornly held to my "no dating until college" resolution for a while. He wasn't bothered. In fact, he seemed only to grow in his steady resolve to patiently woo me and wait. After several months, it occurred to me: *This guy is different. He treats me so… well.* Adam was kind. He respected me, and he was careful with my heart. I began to fall for him. We dated through the last half of my high school years, but early on in college, I suggested taking a break. I thought we should date other people to make sure we weren't committing for life too quickly. He basically said, "You can do that. I'll wait." And I soon realized that I wasn't interested in dating anyone else either.

In addition to our shared faith and calling to ministry, it was Adam's commitment to patiently pursue me that won my heart. His certainty that I was the one for him, and his willingness to wait as long as it took, was both attractive and assuring. On the day before I turned twenty-one, he put a ring on my finger and asked me to marry him. We were two blessed kids—headed toward college graduation, in love, and excited to take on life and ministry together. I'm sure our plans to marry so young seemed crazy to some; after all, for all the good things we had, there were plenty of things we didn't have as well. We didn't have actual experience living in the real world. We didn't have established careers and money. We didn't have our five and ten-year plans mapped out. We didn't have enough hard knocks to know how difficult covenant keeping in a broken world is.

In one sense, Adam and I were very naive going into marriage, but in another sense, we knew all we needed to know at the time. We knew marriage was designed by God and good in his sight. We knew marriage was a covenant for life, not to be entered into lightly. And we knew, in a very theoretical way, that our marriage was bigger than us. So, we set the date and let the planning begin. It was hard to contain our excitement—the wedding day was coming!

Confusing messages

I don't know if there is greater cultural confusion in our world right now than the confusion surrounding marriage and sexuality. As women, we receive a host of mixed messages about these topics from both the world and the church. It's no surprise, then, that far too many Christian women have developed a theology of marriage and sexuality that is woefully incomplete (at best) and wholly unbiblical (at worst).

Since the sexual revolution of the 1960s, women's bodily autonomy has been one golden calf of our secular society. The Bible's ethics are considered outdated and repressive, while freedom from objective morality is touted as the path to true happiness. Our culture says women should be free to sleep with who they want, when they want, without consequences (there's the "my body, my choice" mentality again). If marriage fits into a woman's particular desires for personal fulfillment, great. However, marriage is often viewed as a constraint to women—a union that will stifle her self-expression and success under the demands of home and family.

While much of the secular world says marriage is a prison, and "free love" is the path to flourishing, the church sends a different message. I grew up during the purity culture movement of the 1990s. This movement within Protestant Christianity attempted to counter the sexual revolution by promoting abstinence until marriage. The only teaching on marriage and sexuality I remember receiving at church was this: *True love waits*. Virginity until marriage was the primary goal, and then came the ultimate reward: A husband and wife making it to their wedding night untarnished with a lifetime of amazing sex to follow. While this gets the boundary lines of biblical sexuality right, it is far from a complete picture of what the Bible teaches concerning marriage and sex. By essentially making human marriage ultimate, "true love waits" falls terribly short of revealing the beauty, goodness, and overarching purpose of God's design.

While the church is right to esteem marriage, incomplete theology will not help people face their own relational and sexual brokenness with hope. "True love waits" is not enough for the teenage girl who's sleeping with her boyfriend because she's desperate to believe she's loved right now. Knowing only the Bible's sexual prohibitions doesn't help the young woman in her mid-twenties who struggles with same-sex attraction. It doesn't help the thirty-something-year-old woman who saved herself for marriage but is still single and longing to find "the one." It doesn't offer hope to the fifty-something woman who feels stuck in a marriage full of conflict and pain. And it doesn't comfort the recently widowed sixty-something woman who is grieving the loss of love.

Whether we've internalized unbiblical or partially biblical messages about marriage and sexuality, we all long to be fully known and forever loved by someone who won't shatter our hearts. Without the surety of love like this, we feel unmoored. We cling to human relationships as ultimate sources of identity and security, but it's only in the man Christ Jesus that we find such love. Whether single, dating, married, or single again, the gospel offers us a robust theology of marriage and sexuality from the whole of Scripture. Even better—the gospel invites us into a divine love story that's at the very core of our identity. This love story began before the foundations of the world were laid, but it became visible with the creation of a man and a woman.

Male and female in his image

I was teaching a children's Sunday school class when it struck me just how different boys and girls really are. Each week, I'd give the kids some free-play time before beginning the Bible lesson, and I immediately noticed predictable and contrasting patterns. As the boys arrived, most began constructing weapons of warfare with Legos and K'nex. Then, they ran around the room, chasing one another while engaging in pretend battle. Their boisterousness only escalated until it was time to clean up and begin. The girls had a different routine. Upon arrival, they grabbed a toy or some art supplies and headed for a table. While the boys ran wild, the girls calmly chatted, colored, or put a puzzle together. The gender differences were fascinatingly obvious—and clearly ran deeper than just variances in upbringing!

While biology proves that differences between male and female are undeniable, the Scriptures show that they're *beautiful*. Gender distinction is essential to God's purposes and to ultimate human flourishing. God's good plan for his created world hinges on the reality that human beings are made both male and female in his image (Gen. 1:27–28). In his wisdom, God decided to create, not one, not fifty, but *two* genders through which he would fill the world with his glory. While the man and woman are each fully made in God's likeness, their joint existence— more than that, the union of their differences—enables them to carry out God's plan.

Author Tim Keller says it like this:

> *"In Genesis 1 you see pairs of different but complementary things made to work together: heaven and earth, sea and land, even God and humanity. It is part of the brilliance of God's creation that diverse and unlike things are made to unite and create dynamic wholes which generate more and more life and beauty through their relationships."*[1]

The marriage of Adam and Eve in Genesis 2:24 seems to be the pinnacle demonstration of this unity-within-diversity pattern in God's world. You see, our good God is the originator of gender, sexuality, and marriage. He is the one who thought it up and brought it into existence. God is the one who created the male Adam and then his female complement Eve because "it is not good that the man should be alone" (Gen. 2:18). He is the one who determined that, "a man shall leave his father and his mother and hold fast to his wife, and they shall become one flesh" (Gen. 2:24). But for what purpose? Was Adam's and Eve's marriage (and each marriage since) an end in itself? Once the man and woman had companionship, love, and sexual intimacy with one another, did they experience ultimate fulfillment? Well, no. God created these complementary creatures to live as symbols of a greater reality and to fill the earth through their covenantal, sacrificial, fruitful love. Human sexuality and marriage between man and woman are intended to tell a beautiful story of divine-human love, radical self-giving, and the ultimate union of heaven and earth. If this is true, though, why are the world and the church rife with sexual brokenness, pain, and dysfunction? You probably know the answer by now.

Love gone off the rails

The statistics are staggering and absolutely heartbreaking. One in five girls and one in thirteen boys are sexually abused before the age of eighteen.[2] About two-thirds of Christian and non-Christian men watch pornography at least monthly and divorce rates within and outside of the church range between 40 and 60 percent.[3] Marriage has been trivialized and redefined, sexually transmitted diseases are rampant,[4] gender dysphoria has reached a high among teens,[5] and about 25 percent of American women will have an abortion by the end of their childbearing years.[6] It's not just in statistics that we see this sexual and relational dysfunction. Broken hearts and broken bodies are all around us in real life. We encounter them in our churches, in our families, and in ourselves. Human sexuality has, in effect, gone off the rails.

I recently read an article about a major train derailment in the Midwestern United States. In February 2023, a train crashed in the small town of East Palestine, Ohio, when 38 of its 150 cars derailed and ignited a fire.[7] Trains are designed to run on rails, and if they somehow go off those rails, the result is a disturbance in the normal function of the railway system (at best) and a serious catastrophe (at worst). Similarly, human sexuality is like a train that's gone off the rails for which it was designed, resulting in a major crash and burn. Because we are born with a sin nature that leaves no part of us untouched, all human beings are sexually broken. While the effects of this brokenness vary, the root issue is the same: Human love and sexuality have become self-centered and feelings-driven, rather than God-centered and grounded in objective truth.

The Bible says, "God is love" (1 Jn. 4:8). Our Creator is not simply loving in his behavior, but his nature *is* love. As the very definition of love, God is the only one who rightly determines its moral bounds. But we live in a world that decries the biblical claim "God is love" with the rebuttal "No, *love is love!*" This statement, often used as a slogan for LGBTQ+ rights, comes off as the epitome of kindness and inclusion, but it really just reveals our rebellious grasp at autonomy from God. And seeking autonomy from God in any form always leads to unloving behavior. The rejection of God as the arbiter of true love isn't a new problem, though; it began back in the Garden of Eden. Eve thought she knew better than God what was good, right, and loving, so she took matters into her own hands and disobeyed his word. The consequences have been devastating.

If love can mean anything—if it's untethered from an objective standard—then we must concede that it actually means nothing. At the core, "love is love" means each individual is free to define love as they see fit and do whatever *feels* most loving as a result. The world says if you've fallen out of love with your spouse, you can leave him for someone you *do* feel in love with. If you don't feel attraction to men, you can freely enjoy the romantic and sexual love of a woman. If you don't have a significant other, you can view pornography to get your sexual fix. Sadly, a culture that truly thinks "love is love" is a culture that eventually must approve of everything—from the objectification of image-bearers to the aborting of babies in the womb. When Adam and Eve attempted to redefine love and morality, God's design for sexuality went off the rails like a train rapidly careening off its tracks and igniting a deadly fire. Amid the wreckage, does the gospel offer hope for our broken sexuality? Can the good news of Jesus' self-giving love help us with relational struggles both in singleness and marriage?

Divine love story

In 1990, the romantic comedy *Pretty Woman* came out in theaters. In this risqué version of a Cinderella story, wealthy and ruthless businessman Edward Lewis hires Hollywood prostitute Vivian Ward to stay with him for a week and serve as his escort to several social events. As the week progresses, the two fall in love. Edward begins to treat Vivian more like a lady and romantic interest than a paid sex worker, and Vivian discloses her longing to be rescued, respected, and truly loved. Since the days of her childhood, Vivian has dreamt of a knight on a white horse riding in to save and cherish her forever. Despite their growing love, the pair cannot seem to overcome the complications of their vastly different lives, so Vivian says goodbye and goes home at the end of the week. It doesn't take long for Edward to go after her, though. In a quintessential fairytale ending, Edward arrives at Vivian's apartment in a white limousine. He climbs the fire escape ladder to her window with roses in his teeth, declaring he has come to rescue her with his love.

Pretty Woman saw the highest ever US ticket sales for a romantic comedy.[8] I'm not endorsing the movie; however, it does show that not only do sex and romance sell, but also that the human heart is drawn to love stories of rescue and redemption. Why? In a world where romance and sex have gone off the rails, why do we still long for "happily ever after"? Why do we possess the tiniest shred of hope that it's possible? We yearn for it because we were designed for eternal love and intimacy beyond our wildest imaginings. Sam Allberry writes,

> *"To make sexual freedom our ultimate good is to think that sex and romance is simply an end in itself. But if we realize*

> *that our fascination with romance is actually a memory*
> *trace of a deeper story, an echo of a greater tune, a signpost*
> *to the ultimate destination, then we will find the reality*
> *that can transcend even the most intimate of relationships*
> *we can experience."*[9]

Every good love story is just an echo of history's ultimate love story—the one the Bible tells and the gospel invites us to find ourselves in.

Did you know that human history both begins and ends with a wedding? The book of Genesis recounts the first human marriage and how it quickly went wrong. When Adam and Eve sinned, selfishness, conflict, and power struggles entered their union (Gen. 3:16) and then spread into all human relationships. Since that time, humanity has been on a desperate and futile search for love and intimacy apart from the God in whom we're found. But God has not abandoned his children or given up on his plan to dwell with them.

In the Old Testament, God entered into a relationship of covenant love with his chosen people Israel. He made promises to care for them and live with them forever. Although the people of Israel promised to worship God alone, they were continually unfaithful to him through idol worship. The Bible uses marital language to describe their idolatry, frequently likening them to adulterers (Ezek. 16). And we are no different than Israel. We are spiritual prostitutes, continually running after lovers that cannot ultimately satisfy us. Try as we might, we can't fulfill the deepest longings of our hearts with sex, romance, or even marriage. We need to be rescued from our plight by eternal love, and this is why the gospel is such amazingly good news.

Jesus Christ, who called himself "the bridegroom" (Mk. 2:19) came to earth to redeem for himself an unfaithful bride through the most radical act of self-giving love—death on a cross. Christ gave his life so his bride, the church, might know the acceptance, love, and intimacy with God for which she was made. The story of the Bible concludes in the book of Revelation, looking forward to the final wedding of history—the eternal marriage between Christ and the church. This wedding will take place when Jesus returns to unite heaven and earth in the new creation. He will judge and eradicate evil, gather his bride to himself, and dwell with her in perfection and bliss for all of eternity (Rev. 21:1–3).

If you are in Christ, *beloved bride* is your identity. Although you have union with your Bridegroom now, you are being prepared for the consummation of this eternal marriage—the day Jesus returns bodily and presents "the church to himself in splendor, without spot or wrinkle or any such thing" (Eph. 5:27). But this day often feels so far off, doesn't it? How are we to steward our sexuality and relationships today in light of our final reality? Well, the more we grasp the Bible's divine love story and find ourselves in it, the more it changes the way we live. The gospel gives us eyes to see the goodness of God's sexual ethics, and the purpose of both marriage and singleness.

Human marriage: The signpost of union with Christ

Adam and I got married on an unseasonably warm December day. I remember my dad walking me down the aisle and placing my right hand into Adam's left one. As we stood with our arms interlocked, I vividly recall just how heavy the large bouquet of flowers in my left arm felt—a tangible reminder of the weightiness of what was taking place. Adam's older brother gave the homily from Ephesians 5:22–33, Paul's famous discourse on marriage, because we wanted to declare that our union pointed to something bigger than us. While we understood this theologically, we had a lifetime's worth of growing and learning still ahead—years of allowing our own self-centered conceptions of marriage to be progressively uprooted in everyday life.

In Ephesians 5, Paul gives instructions for Christian marriage. He begins:

> *"Wives, submit to your own husbands, as to the Lord. For the husband is the head of the wife even as Christ is the head of the church, his body, and is himself its Savior. Now as the church submits to Christ, so also wives should submit in everything to their husbands" (Eph. 5:22–23).*

Whoa... hold up. *Submit?!* Because our flesh naturally rails against submission, this verse makes us want to peg Paul as a patriarchal sexist. But let's keep reading:

> *"Husbands, love your wives, as Christ loved the church and gave himself up for her" (Eph. 5:25).*

Paul spends six whole verses instructing husbands to love their wives in a radically sacrificial way. Husbands should lay down their very lives for their wives, just as Christ did for the church.

These verses demonstrate that human marriage is not what the world (and sometimes even the church) says it is. Marriage is neither a hindrance to a woman's fulfillment, nor the means of it. Christ is every woman's true fulfillment! The New Testament reveals that marriage should be a life-long covenant of total self-giving between one man and woman. Marriage is patterned on Christ's redemptive work and points to the believer's unbreakable union with him. When we see that earthly marriage is not the *peak* but the *picture*—the signpost pointing to the ultimate relationship we were made for—it makes the Bible's sexual ethics easier to understand and receive.

So, why, according to Scripture, is sex reserved only for marriage between one man and one woman? Quoting from Genesis, Paul continues:

> "'Therefore a man shall leave his father and mother and hold fast to his wife, and the two shall become one flesh.' This mystery is profound, and I am saying that it refers to Christ and the church" (Eph. 5:31–32).

Author Rebecca McLaughlin sums up the answer well:

> "...if the faithful one-flesh union of a man and a woman pictures Christ's marriage to his church, any sexual relationship outside that model pictures idolatry. Without boundary lines, there is no image."[10]

When we hear the phrase "one flesh union" we tend to think of sex. While the phrase *is* indicative of the sexual union in marriage, it signifies so much more. Tim Keller says sex is a way of doing with your body what you have first done with your whole life:

> "The Bible says don't unite with someone physically unless you are willing to unite with that person emotionally,

personally, socially, economically, and legally. Don't become physically naked and vulnerable to the other person without becoming vulnerable in every other way, because you have given up your freedom and bound yourself in marriage."[11]

We weren't married for long before Adam and I learned that sacrificial, covenant love is hard—*very* hard—for selfish sinners. As two people with very different personalities, very different ways of accomplishing goals, very different ways of handling stress, but a shared natural bent toward selfishness, conflict was inevitable. It's easy to say, "I'm all yours!" at the altar, but total self-giving day by day takes God's grace and our effort, empowered by the Holy Spirit.

Sex was designed by God for the obvious and essential purpose of procreation, but it was also designed to be a physical expression of the total self-giving of marriage. Because the sexual union is powerfully binding, it serves as a commitment mechanism of sorts for the husband and wife bound together in life-long covenant. This design is not only for the good of the couple themselves, but also for the stability of their children and the broader society. Like fire that has powerful benefits within confines, sex is safe and truly good only within its God-given boundaries. Sex is a mutually vulnerable and pleasurable way for married couples to continually say with their bodies, "Because Christ won't walk away from me, I won't walk away from you... Until death do us part."

This understanding of sexuality and marriage was radically counter-cultural in the ancient world, just as it is today. However, the Christian position on singleness was (and is) just as counter-cultural. Christianity has a high view of sex and marriage, but the Bible clearly teaches that human beings don't need them to be happy and whole.

Singleness: The sufficiency of the true Bridegroom

During our seminary years, Adam and I were close friends with a single woman about our age. Although she desired marriage, she was also content in her singleness. She was hard-working, friends with (seemingly) everyone, and a whole lot of fun. Her fervor for serving the Lord and others was both inspiring and contagious. A different friend from college messaged me a couple of years ago expressing discouragement about remaining unmarried in her thirties. Yet despite greatly desiring marriage, she conveyed a deep trust that God was writing a beautiful story with her life, even in her longing. A third friend recently shared the ache of loneliness she sometimes feels as a single woman in a church full of young families. However, she regularly opens her home, welcoming and serving women of all ages, including a lot of tired mamas who need a fun girls' night out. These three women have beautifully modeled a growing security in Christ the true Bridegroom by demonstrating real hope in the eternal marriage to come.

In his wisdom, God has ordained that not all women marry. Many are single for a season, and some are single for life. As with marriage, our views on singleness can be wrongly influenced by both the world and the church, so it's crucial to know what the Bible actually teaches. The Scriptures present both marriage and singleness as gifts from God (1 Cor. 7:7–8). In the ancient Mediterranean world, marriage was extremely important, not for romantic fulfillment, but because family lineage was *everything*. A person's future hope was wholly dependent on the production of a male heir.[12] Considering this, Jesus and Paul (both single) were revolutionary in their affirmation of both marriage *and* celibacy as good, viable ways of life (Matt. 19:3–12 & 1 Cor. 7). Paul and our Lord show us that marriage and the nuclear family are not our ultimate hope—Christ is! The early church demonstrated their belief in this truth by living as a family (Acts 2:44–46) and financially supporting widows who chose not to remarry (1 Tim. 5:3–16).

Our culture says it's good to remain single in order to experience sexual fulfillment apart from the constraints of life-long commitment and sacrifice. In the world's eyes, singleness is for self. The gospels record how Jesus' first disciples evidenced a "singleness for self" mentality as well. In a society where men could divorce their wives for any reason, Jesus reiterated God's design for marriage, (shockingly) permitting divorce only in cases of sexual unfaithfulness (Matt. 19:3–6). When Christ's disciples heard this, they were incredulous and declared that it would be better to remain single than to be trapped in a marriage. In response, Jesus affirmed singleness "for those to whom it is given," not as a means of avoiding the difficulties of commitment but "for the sake of the kingdom of heaven" (Matt. 19:12).

According to the Apostle Paul, believers shouldn't fret about their relationship status because it is good for "each person [to] lead the life that the Lord has assigned to him" (1 Cor. 7:17). While it's good to pursue marriage (for the right reasons), it is also good to remain single as a means of securing "undivided devotion to the Lord" (1 Cor. 7:35). Paul reminds believers that everything in this life—including marriage—is passing away (1 Cor. 7:29, 31). We are rapidly moving toward an eternity where humans "neither marry nor are given in marriage" (Matt. 22:30) because the ultimate marriage will be consummated. When Jesus returns to claim his bride, there will be no need for marriage and sex as we now know them because the signs will give way to the reality of the ultimate marriage. It's this ultimate union that infuses both Christian marriage and Christian singleness with great purpose. Author Juli Slattery says it well:

> *"While God created sexual desire to awaken our longing for love, even marriage is not the ultimate fulfillment of that desire. Marriage is the shadow, the foretaste, the metaphor of the true longing to be known, embraced, accepted, and celebrated by our Creator."*[13]

This means "celibacy for the kingdom is not a rejection of sexuality. It is a call to embrace the ultimate meaning and purpose of sexuality, knowing the one flesh union is only a foreshadowing of something infinitely more grand and glorious."[14]

Single and married Christians alike are to faithfully tell the gospel story with their lives, but they tell it from two different angles. Marriage reveals the shape of the gospel by picturing our covenant relationship with Christ. Singleness reveals the sufficiency of the gospel by showing that our relationship with Christ is ultimate.[15] Christian singleness, both in the ancient world and today, is a demonstration that our true hope is found in union with Christ and membership in God's family.

Summing it up

I wonder if you're thinking all this sounds wonderful but far too idealistic to help you today. Sure, this may be what marriage and singleness are *supposed* to represent, but the reality is often not pretty. Maybe you're in a marriage filled with conflict and struggle, and you find it very difficult to respect and submit to your husband. Maybe you've experienced the pain of unfaithfulness, abandonment, abuse, or divorce. Maybe you've been single for years, and you long for a spouse and children. Perhaps you've hopped from one romantic relationship to the next looking for satisfaction. Or maybe you're tempted to idolize your marriage, believing it's all you need. In each of these situations and numerous others, there are no quick fixes or easy solutions this side of heaven. But the gospel offers you deep and unshakeable hope! Your Bridegroom Jesus Christ stands ready to forgive you for all the ways you have failed to obediently steward your sexuality for his good purposes. He stands ready to heal you from the damage relational sin has wrought in your life. He is eager to sustain and satisfy you in himself, transforming your earthly relationships into beautiful trophies of his grace. Run to him in repentance and faith. Acknowledge that he is enough. Surrender your sexuality totally to him. Seek practical help from trusted members of his body for your own relational and sexual struggles.

Jesus Christ, the lover of your soul, can be trusted with your vulnerable heart. He is a Bridegroom who longs to lavish you with his love and affection, who will never leave or forsake you, who is preparing a place for you to dwell with him forever. Amid all that is not right, you can live with great anticipation and joy: The wedding day is coming!

Questions for reflection and discussion

1. What are some messages the world sends regarding romance, sexuality, and marriage? How is the teaching "True love waits" on its own not enough to counter the world's message?

2. Read Genesis 1:27–28 and Ephesians 5:31–32. Explain how God's creation of male and female image-bearers is essential to his purposes to fill the world with his glory and redeem it from sin.

3. Describe some of the ways love and sex have "gone off the rails" in our world and in your own life. Why should Christians teach that "God is love" rather than "love is love"?

4. The Bible tells a divine love story which begins and ends with a wedding. How does this story help us see God's boundaries for human sexuality as purposeful and good rather than arbitrary and cruel?

5. Read Ephesians 5:22–33. Describe how the union of one man and one woman for life is intended to image Christ's relationship with the church. How does understanding human marriage as a temporary signpost affect our understanding of singleness (see 1 Cor. 7:25–35)?

6. Whether you are single, dating, married, or single again, have you completely submitted your sexuality and relationships to the lordship of your true Bridegroom? Discuss or jot down some practical ways that you can turn to him for help, healing, and growth in your relationships.

7. Both marriage and singleness are gifts from God. Each state comes with its own hardships and advantages. What are some practical ways you can encourage both your married and single sisters in Christ to faithfully steward their sexuality and relationships for the sake of the Kingdom?

10

Women of War

Changing the world in the strength of the Lord

Finally, be strong in the Lord and in the strength of
his might. Put on the whole armor of God, that you
may be able to stand against the schemes of the devil.
For we do not wrestle against flesh and blood, but
against the rulers, against the authorities, against
the cosmic powers over this present darkness, against
the spiritual forces of evil in the heavenly places.
—Ephesians 6:10–12

I was thirteen years old when I realized I wanted to change the world. I don't think I said those words out loud, but I remember feeling an overwhelming desire to do something that really mattered—something that would impact others for good and help push back the darkness. I didn't want to be famous or rich, but I did want my life to count for something bigger than me. At a youth retreat in January 2000, I felt the Holy Spirit nudging me toward vocational Christian ministry. Although I had no idea what that would look like, I couldn't see myself doing anything else with my life.

The desire to do something world-changing became very pronounced again around the time of my high school graduation. In a speech at my commencement ceremony, I implored my classmates to leave a legacy that would last into eternity, reminding them that we each have just one life to live, and only what's done in service to Christ will endure. Admittedly, this was a somewhat unusual topic for a graduation speech, but I knew it was important (and in a Bible-belt small town in the early 2000s, no one openly balked). I wanted to do great things for God, and I wanted others to join me.

It didn't take long, however, for me to realize that I'm not strong or capable enough to do great things for God. As a goal-oriented high achiever, I'm tempted to believe the lie that my worth comes from what I accomplish and how well I accomplish it. As a result of my personality and particular sin proclivities, I don't manage stress well. In high school, I struggled with body image and an eating disorder. In college, I faced seasons of anxiety and depression, which required medication. These trials became intense again during the postpartum days of motherhood, and I still struggle with bouts of them today.

These limitations—my particular sins and sufferings—continually remind me that victory in the Christian life, much less changing the world, is utterly impossible in my own strength. However, when I view my own weaknesses (and the weaknesses of those God has used throughout history) through the lens of the gospel, I see that world-changing in the kingdom of God looks quite different than what we often imagine.

World-changers: Saints and soldiers

We are living in the digital age of social media, influencers, and "fast fame." Many women are creating brands, building platforms, sharing life hacks, and rocking side-hustles. In the evangelical world, Christian women are sharing truth through creative content, and growing an online following in the process. While these certainly have the potential to be Christ-exalting and kingdom-building, it's easy to believe this is the primary work of world-changing. As we scroll, it can seem like the women who are publicly producing, achieving, and being followed, liked, and shared are the ones really making a difference.

In addition, we tend to think those who do "extraordinary" things for God are the real world-changers—the foreign missionaries, the big-name Bible teachers, the church leaders, the super Christians. But are there such things as super Christians, and by default average and subpar Christians? The Bible makes no such distinctions among those who are in Christ. To the contrary, Paul demonstrates in Ephesians that all believers are both saints and soldiers—a redeemed army through whom God is changing the world.

In our minds a saint is a spiritual elite (a super-Christian), but Paul uses the term throughout his entire letter to refer to *all* who are in Christ (Eph. 1:1). People from every tribe, tongue, and nation, who have been redeemed by Jesus and set apart as holy for God's purposes are *saints*. The saints comprise the church, and the church is God's chosen vehicle for getting the gospel message—the good news of Jesus' salvation—to every part of the world. As the church carries out this mission, God is saving souls, transforming lives, and revealing his plan to renew the whole of creation by uniting all things in Christ (Eph. 1:10). This plan captures the attention of supernatural beings, as it's "through the church [that] the manifold wisdom of God might now be made known to the rulers and authorities in the heavenly places" (Eph. 3:10).

Both God's allies and his enemies in the spiritual realm are keenly aware of what he is doing in the world through his church, but these spiritual forces of good and evil respond quite differently. When the angels of light see God's purposes being worked out through his people, they worship him (1 Pet. 1:12, Rev. 7:11). In contrast, when the demonic forces see it, they violently rage against the church, attempting to thwart God's plan (1 Pet. 5:8, Eph. 6:12).

For this reason, the climax of Ephesians is a call to arms:

> "Put on the whole armor of God, that you may be able to stand against the schemes of the devil. For we do not wrestle against flesh and blood, but against the rulers, against the authorities, against the cosmic powers over this present darkness, against the spiritual forces of evil in the heavenly places" (Eph. 6:11–12).

Paul makes it clear that every saint is also a soldier in an intense spiritual war. The problem, however, is that few Christian women in the West view themselves as either saints or soldiers. When it comes to our sense of identity, we rarely equate being *in Christ* with being a soldier, especially if we've lived relatively comfortable lives devoid of persecution and the horrors of physical war.

Unwise to the war
In the preface to *The Screwtape Letters*, C.S. Lewis writes:

"There are two equal and opposite errors into which our race can fall about the devils. One is to disbelieve in their existence. The other is to believe, and to feel an excessive and unhealthy interest in them. They themselves are equally pleased with both errors…"[1]

In the West—where we value what can be seen, touched, and measured—the first error is the greater danger for many. Sure, those of us who grew up in church would likely say we believe in angels, demons, and spiritual warfare. But we often function as if they don't really exist. Many Christian women operate in total oblivion to the spiritual war being waged over their own minds and hearts.

What comes to mind when you think about conflict and war? Perhaps you ponder the combat between nations throughout history and the problems of violence, crime, racism, and poverty. Maybe you picture soldiers in the military deploying to fight. Perhaps the culture wars between political parties and those with differing ideologies come to mind. Notions of war might even trigger thoughts about the arguments you experience in your personal life.

When Paul says we don't wrestle with flesh and blood (Eph. 6:12), he isn't denying the realities of human discord and evil. Rather, he is alerting the people of God to our invisible reality: We are soldiers in a war of cosmic proportions—*the* war behind all the visible conflict we see and experience in our world. This war is not physical, ideological, or cultural—it's spiritual. And our primary enemies are not human. Timothy Gombis sums it up well: "The enemy in the church's warfare is not the world or the people in the world but the powers."[2]

Seriously? The *powers?* This sounds crazy to those of us trained by our culture to envisage the devil as a cartoon-like figure with a red suit, pitchfork, and horns. What kind of enemy is that? Certainly not one to fear! In a world full of numerous visible problems, we have bigger things to worry about than an invisible war with this character. But the Bible corrects our inaccurate conceptions of the powers of darkness.

God has a very real and dangerous enemy, who has temporarily been allowed great sway over our darkened world (1 Jn. 5:19). This enemy hates God's Son, despises the church, and wants to subvert God's mission in the world. He is intelligent and crafty, known as "the father of lies" (Gen. 3:1; Jn. 8:44). Although he is full of cruelty and pride, he disguises himself as a beautiful angel of light (2 Cor. 11:14–15). He knows the cross and resurrection of Christ sealed his ultimate defeat (Col. 2:15; Rev. 20:10), and this infuriates him. So, he prowls around like a roaring lion, looking for people to devour with doubt, discouragement, and despair (1 Pet. 5:8). While Satan cannot ultimately destroy those who are in Christ (Jn. 10:27–29), he would love nothing more than to make the saints miserable. He aims to render us ineffective for God's kingdom.

Paul spent the first five chapters of Ephesians expounding the purposes of God through the church. Now he urges believers to wake up and wise up to the enemy who wants to foil those purposes. Ephesians 6 is the climax of the entire letter and a clarion call to fight, so "that you may be able to stand against the schemes of the devil" (Eph. 6:11). To be a Christian woman means to actively engage in spiritual combat. Unfortunately, though, our fallen and frail humanity renders us unequally matched to our supernatural opponents.

Unequal to the battle: Sinners and sufferers

I live with four boys, which means *a lot* of horseplay and wrestling happen within the walls of my home. My middle two sons, John Wicks and Nate, are both athletic, but at this point in life they are unequally matched wrestling opponents because John Wicks is significantly larger than Nate. Despite Nate's strength and athleticism, he's the underdog when tussling with his older brother. Unless, of course, Nate wrestles with the help of his dad, who is much bigger and stronger. If Nate can convince Dad to wrestle on his team, John Wicks doesn't stand a chance.

In a similar way, we wrestle with a supernatural enemy who is far more powerful than us. Yes, *in Christ* we are saints and soldiers, but we are also sinners and sufferers living in a fallen world. This means life is hard... very hard. Satan is aware of the specific trials and sin patterns that plague each of us, and he plays to our weaknesses with great skill. While the particulars look different in each person's life, the enemy's overarching strategy is the same: Through temptations and accusations, Satan attempts to twist our view of God and of self. In temptation, Satan *inflates* our view of self by whispering the lies: *Only you know what's right and good for you. Listen to your own heart! Trust your feelings and do what you want.* He strokes our pride, directing our gaze to the world's pleasures and enticing us to disobey our Creator. In accusation, Satan *deflates* our view of self by whispering different lies: *You've really blown it now! God can't possibly forgive you for falling into that same ol' sin again. You might as well give up.* These accusations coax us toward self-loathing, an inverse form of pride that leads us to dwell excessively on ourselves, minimizing Christ's sacrifice.[3]

In my own life, Satan regularly tempts me to distrust God for financial provision. Because Adam and I are in vocational ministry, we've never had an abundance of money. Although God has always been *so* faithful to provide what we and our four boys need (and beyond), I regularly find myself anxious about finances. In his Word, God expressly tells me not to worry but to seek first his kingdom, trusting him to meet my needs (Matt. 6:31–33). Satan, however, loves tempting me to doubt God. He whispers, *Wow, those boys are getting expensive as they grow! How are you going to pay for such-and-such as they get older? How will you keep doing what you feel called to do and make it financially? It sure looks like God isn't going to come through this time. You should have chosen a different profession, then you wouldn't have to depend on God so much!* I'm ashamed to say I have spent many nights endlessly fretting rather than trusting in my generous and faithful God.

Then, in seasons when I am facing the lows of depression, Satan loves to throw stinging darts of accusation at me. His voice hisses: *Here you go again, you irrational weakling. You're acting totally crazy! If you were really a Christian, you wouldn't feel so down and out. Where is your Christ-like joy and peace? You fake! What would people from church think if they saw you crying like this? You're a mess. You're a burden to your family....*

The enemy will go to great lengths to get us doubting God and believing lies about our identity. He will do whatever it takes to keep us from resting in the gospel and to prevent us from sharing it with others. If the enemy can keep us navel-gazing—wallowing in puddles of self-loathing and self-pity—he can discourage and distract us from the world-changing mission we've been given. On our own, we are no match for Satan; we are far too weak, and he is far too cunning. This would be cause for despair were we not joined to one who is infinitely stronger than our adversary

(1 Jn. 4:4). The glorious truth is that we are *in Christ*—united by faith to the sinless Son of God, who triumphed over evil through weakness. So, don't despair! Through Christ and his resources, we can stand against the schemes of the devil. Satan wants to use our weaknesses and sins to keep us from enduring until the end, but God wants to use them to transform us into humble, righteous people—people who change the world as we cling to Christ in faith. In a mind-blowing paradox, God's power works best in our weakness (2 Cor. 12:9), which is why Paul commands all sinner-sufferer-soldier-saints to "be strong in the Lord and in the strength of his might" (Eph. 6:10).

Divine Warrior

When I consider famous war stories, the battle between David and Goliath immediately comes to mind. As the story goes, God's chosen people Israel are up against the Philistines but have reached a stalemate. Goliath of Gath, a literal giant, comes out with chest-thumping arrogance and an impressive suit of armor to fight any champion Israel will put forward on their behalf. Saul, the king of Israel, and his entire army are shaking in their boots. No one is courageous enough to face Goliath until David, the shepherd boy from Bethlehem, bravely steps up to fight the giant with only a sling and five smooth stones. In an amazing turn of events, David takes Goliath down with a stone to the forehead, then proceeds to use the giant's own sword to chop off his head. Through David, Israel was victorious.

When this story is retold, listeners are usually encouraged to think of themselves as David and emulate his courage: *Be brave like David and fight your giants!* The reality, however, is that we're all more like Israel—paralyzed by fear and weakness, and needful of someone to fight on our behalf. David's own words in the biblical account reveal that God is the true hero of the story. The shepherd boy is only a representative, fighting in the strength of the Divine Warrior. He says to Goliath:

> "This day the LORD will deliver you into my hand... that all this assembly may know that the LORD saves not with sword and spear. For the battle is the LORD's, and he will give you into our hand" (1 Sam. 17:46–47).

The story of David and Goliath is one among numerous accounts in the Old Testament where God fights for Israel, and God doesn't just fight their physical battles; he also fights their greater spiritual battles. In Isaiah 59, the prophet depicts God as a divine warrior, stepping in to save his people from their sin when no one else can:

> "He [the LORD] saw that there was no man, and wondered that there was no one to intercede; then his own arm brought him salvation, and his righteousness upheld him. He put on righteousness as a breastplate, and a helmet of salvation on his head" (Is. 59:16–17).

What an incredible picture of God and—even more—his Christ! Jesus is the divine-human warrior, who interceded for us by crushing the head of the serpent through his death and resurrection.

When Paul tells saints to "be strong in the Lord" and "put on the whole armor of God" (Eph. 6:10–11), he seems to be writing from a mind steeped in Isaiah's portrayal of God as the Divine

Warrior. Paul's exhortation to "take up the whole armor of God, that you may be able to withstand in the evil day" (Eph. 6:13) is a call for the church to follow Christ by continuing the fight against the powers of darkness in *his* strength.

What does this fight look like in our everyday lives? Certainly not violent words and militant aggression toward those who disagree with us. We don't fight the enemy with his own weapons of lies, hatred, and anger. Rather, we fight with humility, repentance of sin, obedience to God, and the cross-shaped faithfulness of a progressively transformed life. We wage war just as Christ did—through death and resurrection. As we die daily to our stubborn, remaining sins and are raised by the Spirit to new ways of living, we proclaim the victory of Christ over the darkness. Our fight looks less like militancy and more like getting dressed, as we put on the armor Christ first wore for us—the armor of God's virtuous character.[4]

Suit up: No sundresses and heels!

I have always loved clothes, shoes, and any chance to get dressed up. When I was a little girl, I often played in my mom's slips and dresses. I once even asked a stranger in a restaurant if I could wear the red shoes she had on her feet. In high school and college, I thoroughly enjoyed picking out formal dresses to wear to proms and events, and during seminary I worked retail at a high-end women's clothing store where I was able to buy nice clothes at a very discounted price. These days, I don't have as many opportunities to wear sundresses and heels. I'm a busy mom, constantly on the move. When I'm running errands, keeping our home, and caring for kids, t-shirts and athletic wear are the most practical clothing choices.

As women, we know how to dress appropriately for where we're going and what we're doing each day. Just as we wouldn't wear a bathrobe and slippers to a formal event, we wouldn't wear a nice dress and high heels to go for a jog. However, when it comes to getting dressed *spiritually*, we don't tend to have as much discernment about what to wear. In Ephesians 6, Paul makes it clear that, because we are soldiers, we need to intentionally "dress" our minds and hearts for battle. Metaphorically speaking, a cute sundress and sandals will not do if we are to withstand Satan's assaults. We need heavy, protective covering to persevere in the Christian life and fulfill God's purposes in the world. We need the very armor of God.

In Ephesians 6:14–17, Paul lists six pieces of spiritual armor. This suit of armor represents God's character, exhibited perfectly in Jesus' humanity and saving work. To say it another way, the armor of God is the gospel. Through our union with Christ by faith, God's character is already ours, but we must daily put it on and fight. We don the armor as we live in accordance with our identity in Christ. This is what it means to "put on the Lord Jesus Christ, and make no provision for the flesh, to gratify its desires" (Rom 13:14). When we hear the term "spiritual warfare" we tend to think of something strange and mysterious, but engaging in spiritual warfare is simply holding fast to our gospel convictions through all of life's ups and downs.[5] What are these gospel convictions we must hold if we are to stand against the enemy? We find them in the six pieces of spiritual armor.

Belt of truth

> *"Stand therefore, having fastened on the belt of truth"*
> *(Eph. 6:14).*

172

In our sin, we "exchanged the truth about God for a lie" (Rom. 1:25) and were "corrupt through deceitful desires" (Eph. 4:22). Yet, even when we loved deception, God's Divine Warrior Jesus came to save us with truth as his supportive belt. He called himself "the way, the truth, and the life" (Jn. 14:6), and in him alone we discover and become our truest selves. Gospel truth is the belt supporting our core identity, holding every other piece of the armor together. We wage war against the enemy by daily renewing our minds in the Scriptures, taking our thoughts captive (2 Cor. 10:5) and responding to Satan's deceitful temptations and accusations with gospel truth. In my case, I fasten up the belt of truth by reminding myself that if God has provided for my greatest need (salvation from sin), then he *can* and *will* certainly be faithful to meet my physical and financial needs (Rom. 8:32). When I fall into the sins of worry and lack of faith, I must renew my mind in the truth that I stand fully forgiven in Christ and need only to repent and look to him.

Breastplate of righteousness

> "...and having put on the breastplate of righteousness"
> (Eph. 6:14).

In our sin, we had no righteousness of our own (Rom. 3:10–12). Even our "good" works were like filthy rags to God (Is. 64:6) because they came from an unrighteous heart rather than faith (Rom. 14:23). But God's Divine Warrior Jesus put on his righteousness like a breastplate to save us (Is. 59:17). In a great exchange, the righteous Son of God took our sin upon himself that we might receive his righteousness (2 Cor. 5:21). We battle

Satan by remembering that we stand in the righteousness of Christ alone, and his indwelling Spirit empowers our righteous deeds as a result.

Gospel of peace

> "...and, as shoes for your feet, having put on the readiness given by the gospel of peace" (Eph. 6:15).

Our sin left us estranged from God as his enemies (Eph. 2:12). And having no peace with him, we also lacked inner peace. But when Jesus came to earth, the angels announced that he came to bring peace to those God favors (Lk. 2:14). Jesus became our peace (Eph. 2:14), reconciling all who believe back to God and to each other. One day he will bring total world peace as he quells the rebellion of all God's enemies. When our feet run to proclaim the good news of salvation—sharing the gospel with a neighbor over coffee, with a stranger on an airplane, or with our kids at the dinner table—we wage war against the powers of evil.

Shield of faith

> "In all circumstances take up the shield of faith, with which you can extinguish all the flaming darts of the evil one" (Eph. 6:16).

Apart from Christ, we had nothing to protect us from the righteous wrath our sins deserve, but God provided a shield for us in his Son (Ps. 5:11–12). We take up this shield by faith as we trust Jesus alone for eternal protection. We wage war against Satan's fiery arrows as we walk by faith through temptations and trials, clinging to God's promises. And we continually remind ourselves of every spiritual blessing that is ours in Christ (Eph. 1:3): We are chosen, loved, forgiven, and secure, and nothing can take that away.

Helmet of salvation

"...and take the helmet of salvation" (Eph. 6:17).

Apart from Christ, we were spiritually dead (Eph. 2:1) and separated from God (Is. 59:2). No one else could rescue us from this plight, so God himself put on a helmet of salvation and came for us (Is. 59:17). We fight the enemy by resting in Christ alone for salvation, remembering that his work is effective for the past, the present, and the future. We have been justified (saved from the penalty of sin), we are being sanctified (saved from the power of sin), and we will be glorified (saved from the presence of sin). So, when Satan whispers *you're not good enough* we can respond: "No, but Jesus is!"

Sword of the Spirit

"...and the sword of the Spirit, which is the word of God"
(Eph. 6:17).

Apart from Christ, we had no desire or power to fight the enemy or our sin. But when the gospel message came to us, it came in power through the Holy Spirit (1 Thes. 1:5). God's convicting

Word is living, active, and sharper than a sword (Heb. 4:12). It never returns void but always accomplishes the purpose for which it was sent (Is. 55:11). Jesus himself is the living Word of God (Jn. 1:1), and he used the written Word to resist Satan's temptations in the wilderness (Matt. 4:1–11). We fight the enemy by following his example. *Women of war are women of the Word*—saturating their minds in Scripture daily and wisely wielding its truths to combat the evil one. This is dynamic warfare that not only changes us but also changes the world as God's kingdom comes on earth.

Summing it up

I was pulling out of a parking lot when a bumper sticker caught my attention. It said, "Well-behaved women rarely make history." I googled the quote and found it was a popular slogan for mugs and stickers, presumably because of its implied message: To leave their mark on the world, women must rebel against conventions. The earliest version of the quote is attributed to historian Laurel Thatcher Ulrich, who actually wrote, "well-behaved women seldom make history." When read in context, it's clear Ulrich was not implying women should misbehave in order to be remembered. Rather, she was lamenting the fact that so many virtuous women remain unknown despite the necessary and valuable contributions they've made to society.[6] But just because a woman isn't *known* by the world doesn't mean she isn't *changing* it.

As Christian women, we don't change the world by rebelling against conventional morality or by striving in our own strength to do impressive things for God. In a way that seems totally counterintuitive, we make a mark that echoes into eternity by faithfully and humbly persevering in the ordinary Christian life until the end. We change the world by becoming gospel-shaped women through and through. This means daily accepting a posture of weakness, admitting our desperate need, and resting in the good news of the gospel by faith. It means finding our true identity and worth in being united to Jesus and embracing all the spiritual benefits that are ours in him. It means knowing and depending upon the Holy Spirit as our source of power for godly living and finding our true belonging in God's family—the church. It means letting our new identity transform the way we think and live in every area—in our work, in our friendships, in how we use our bodies, in our marriage or singleness, and in our on-going battles with Satan, sin, and suffering.

The goal of a Christian woman is not to be remembered but to faithfully serve a Savior who will never be forgotten. Our names may not be in the history books, but when our identity is rooted in the hero of history, we become part of his world-wide, eternal legacy that cannot be frustrated. As we rest in Christ and learn to live all of life for him, he transforms us in ways that not only subvert the powers of darkness but also build a kingdom that cannot be shaken (Heb. 12:28). Christ is reconciling the world to himself and making all things new so, sisters, be strong in the Lord and the strength of his might! This is gospel-shaped womanhood, and this...? Well, it changes everything—all to the praise of his glorious grace.

Questions for reflection and discussion

1. As you consider your life, how do you want it to count and make a difference in the world? Do you tend to assume world-changing is the work of well-known influencers and

"super Christians"?

2. What does it mean that every believer is both a saint and a soldier? When you consider your identity in Christ, do you think of yourself as a saint? A soldier? Why or why not?

3. Read Ephesians 6:10–13. Christians can either be unaware of Satan or become too focused on him. How does this passage help us strike a proper balance in thinking about the supernatural powers? In what ways do you need to wake up to the unseen war?

4. The Bible calls Satan "the Father of lies." Describe how he plays to the sins you're most prone to through specific temptations and accusations.

5. Read Ephesians 6:14–17. Choose one of the six pieces of armor Paul lists and describe how it reflects the character of God and the gospel. Which piece of armor brings you the most comfort?

6. Explain how waging war against the enemy is like getting dressed spiritually. Practically speaking, how do we put on the armor and fight? Pick one piece of the armor and describe what it would look like for you to put it on and wage war.

7. To be a gospel-shaped woman is to daily renew our minds in our Christian identity and then allow that identity to drive all we do in life. Which chapter from Part 1 of this book was most helpful in giving you a better understanding of who you are *in Christ*? Discuss or jot down how this understanding is changing the way you live in one area of life, perhaps by picking a topic from Part 2.

Acknowledgements

Many are the plans in the mind of a man, but it is the
purpose of the LORD that will stand.
—*Proverbs 19:21*

Writing and publishing a book is a humbling endeavor. It's
something I've always dreamt of doing, but thought I likely never
would. The Lord had other plans, though. What a faith-building
journey it has been to watch him sovereignly orchestrate all the
details of this project. He used a number of people, places, and
circumstances in my life at just the right time to make this book
a reality, and I am eternally grateful.

To begin, I would not have had the theological knowledge
or the strong desire to write this book without my time at The
Southern Baptist Theological Seminary. My love for the gospel
(and my understanding that it is good news, not just for eternity,
but also for life today) really blossomed during my years at
Southern. I am so thankful for Dr. Albert Mohler's leadership
and for the many professors who shaped my thinking through
their teaching.

To all the friends and acquaintances who have read my blog
(and microblog on social media) over the past decade and
encouraged me to keep using my gifts for the glory of God,

thank you. Without you, there would be no *Gospel-Shaped Womanhood.*

I am grateful for Nancy Guthrie, who I providentially connected with on Instagram of all places. Nancy championed my writing and introduced me to Jonathan Carswell, CEO of 10ofThose. I am grateful for Jonathan and the team at 10Publishing, who took a chance on a first-time author and published *Tracing Glory* in 2021. I'm also grateful for Brad Byrd, who repeatedly encouraged me to send in more ideas and write a second book. His prompting propelled me forward in this project. Many thanks to my editor, Sheri Newton, who offered such a great balance of encouragement and helpful critique. You are a joy to work with and made this book better. I'm also grateful for Jonathan Pountney, Lois Ferguson, and Beth Lees at 10Publishing, along with designer Jude May.

To John Sloan, my husband Adam, Chris Moncrief, and the entire elder team at Capshaw Baptist Church, thank you for ensuring that my mind and heart are saturated in gospel-centered preaching, teaching, and worship week after week. Your faithfulness and skill in proclaiming the good news is a gift that has truly shaped me—and one I don't take for granted.

To my friends Chrissy, Dahisy, and Megan, thank you for praying for me, encouraging me, and listening to me talk about this project for two years! Megan, thank you for using your formatting skills and attention to detail to help put the manuscript together. I am grateful for each of you.

To my parents and in-laws, I cannot thank you enough for investing so generously in your grandchildren's lives and giving me extended writing time in the process. Your love and support have been crucial to this project. All four of you are truly the best.

Finally, to the five guys who sacrificed the most to make this book a reality, I am so grateful. Adam, you've faithfully loved me at my best and my worst. Thank you for being so excited about my writing opportunities, for solo parenting multiple days to give me undistracted writing time, and for not letting me quit when I felt overwhelmed. I truly could not have done this without you. Luke, John Wicks, Nate, and Cameron, you have given me so much grace during this year when my plate has been very full. Thank you for being proud of my books (so proud that you want to knock on doors and sell them to our neighbors), and for always being so generous with your love and affection. You may never read this book, but I pray that you and your dad are the five people most influenced by it as I seek to live what I've written. By God's grace, may all six of us be gospel-shaped. I love you dearly.

Endnotes

Chapter 1

1. The Editors of Encyclopaedia Britannica, "Gospel: New Testament" in Encyclopaedia Britannica, May 15, 2023, https://www.britannica.com/topic/Gospel-New-Testament.
2. MacArthur, John, *The MacArthur New Testament Commentary: Ephesians* (Moody Publishers, 1986) 53.
3. Doyle, Glennon, *Untamed* (The Dial Press, 2020) 59.
4. Allberry, Sam, *Is God Anti-Gay?: And Other Questions about Homosexuality, the Bible and Same-Sex Attraction* (The Good Book Company, 2015) 11–12.
5. Keller, Timothy, *The Meaning of Marriage: Facing the Complexities of Commitment with the Wisdom of God* (Penguin Books, 2011) 44.

Chapter 2

1. Haynam, Josh, *22 Examples of High Converting Quizzes Used for Facebook Marketing*, accessed May 31, 2023, https://www.tryinteract.com/blog/22-examples-of-high-converting-quizzes-used-for-facebook-marketing.
2. Anderson, Hannah, "Reflection: Made in God's Image" in *Identity Theft*, edited by Melissa Kruger (The Gospel Coalition, 2018) 19–20.
3. Wilbourne, Rankin, *Union with Christ: The Way to Know and Enjoy God* (David C. Cook, 2016) 155.
4. Dodds, Abigail, *(A)Typical Woman: Free, Whole, and Called in Christ* (Crossway, 2019) 33.

5. Henry, Matthew, *Volume VI: Acts to Revelation*, Matthew Henry's Commentary on the Whole Bible (Fleming H. Revell Company) 687.

6. Boice, James Montgomery, *Ephesians, An Expositional Commentary* (Baker Books, 1997) 6.

7. Ibid.

8. Gombis, Timothy G., *The Drama of Ephesians: Participating in the Triumph of God* (InterVarsity Press, 2010) 68–69.

9. Piper, John, "Children, Heirs, and Fellow Sufferers," *Desiring God Blog*, April 21, 2002, https://www.desiringgod.org/messages/children-heirs-and-fellow-sufferers.

Chapter 3

1. McLaughlin, Rebecca, *The Secular Creed: Engaging Five Contemporary Claims* (The Gospel Coalition, 2021) 66.

2. Ibid. 67.

3. Ibid. 69.

4. Merkle, Rebekah, "Throw Like a Girl: Why Feminism Insults Real Women," *Desiring God Blog*, March 3, 2017, https://www.desiringgod.org/articles/throw-like-a-girl.

5. Boice, James Montgomery, *Ephesians, An Expositional Commentary* (Baker Books, 1997) 32.

6. Gombis, Timothy G., *The Drama of Ephesians: Participating in the Triumph of God* (InterVarsity Press, 2010) 68.

7. Boice, James Montgomery, *Ephesians, An Expositional Commentary* (Baker Books, 1997) 37.

Chapter 4

1. "Need to Belong," *Psychology*, January 11, 2016, http://psychology.iresearchnet.com/social-psychology/interpersonal-relationships/need-to-belong.

2. Allison, Gregg R., *The Church: An Introduction* (Crossway, 2021) 23.

3. Grudem, Wayne, *Systematic Theology: An Introduction to Biblical Doctrine* (Zondervan Academic, 1994) 853.

4. Dever, Mark, *The Church: The Gospel Made Visible* (B&H Publishing Group, 2012) 16.

5. Hill, Megan, *A Place to Belong: Learning to Love the Local Church* (Crossway, 2020) 104.

6. Erickson, Millard J., *Christian Theology* (Baker Academic, 1998) 1043.

7. Flavel, John, *All Things Made New: John Flavel for the Christian Life*, edited by Lewis Allen (The Banner of Truth Trust, 2017) 254.

Chapter 5

1. Greear, J.D., "Gospel Above All," *J.D. Greear Ministries*, March 12, 2018, https://jdgreear.com/gospel-above-all.

2. MacArthur, John, *The MacArthur New Testament Commentary: Ephesians* (Moody Publishers, 1986) 119.

3. Boice, James Montgomery, *Ephesians, An Expositional Commentary* (Baker Books, 1997) 122.

4. Schaeffer, Francis, *True Spirituality: How to Live for Jesus Moment by Moment* (Tyndale House Publishers, 2001) 66.

5. Butterfield, Kent, "Putting Off and Putting On," *Table Talk Blog*, July 3, 2019, https://tabletalkmagazine.com/posts/putting-off-and-putting-on-2019-06.

6. Boice, James Montgomery, *Ephesians, An Expositional Commentary* (Baker Books, 1997) 166–167.

7. McKelvey, Douglas, *Every Moment Holy*, Vol. 1 (Rabbit Room Press, 2017) 4.

Chapter 6

1. Keller, Timothy, *Every Good Endeavor: Connecting Your Work to God's Work* (Penguin Books, 2014) 63.

2. Huff, Larry, "How the Reformation Changed the Culture and Why It Still Matters Today," *Yellowhammer*, October 31, 2017, https://yellowhammernews.com/reformation-changed-culture-still-matters-today/.

3. Chesterton, G.K., "The Emancipation of Domesticity," in *What's*

Wrong With the World, EBook #1717, Last updated: October 9, 2016, https://www.gutenberg.org/files/1717/1717-h/1717-h.htm#link2H_4_0021.

Chapter 7

1. Edwards, Jonathan, *The Miscellanies*, 1153–1360, The Works of Jonathan Edwards Series, Vol. 23 (Yale University Press, 2004) 23:350, quoted in "You Won't Make It Alone: Five Reasons You Need Good Friends," *Desiring God Blog*, September 24, 2018, https://www.desiringgod.org/articles/you-wont-make-it-alone.

2. Hellerman, Joseph H., *When the Church Was a Family: Recapturing Jesus' Vision for Authentic Christian Community* (B&H Academic, 2009) 67, 79, 83.

3. Ibid. 77, 83.

4. Keller, Timothy, *The Freedom of Self-Forgetfulness: The Path to True Christian Joy* (10Publishing, 2012) 32.

Chapter 8

1. Pearcey, Nancy R., *Love Thy Body: Answering Hard Questions About Life and Sexuality* (Baker Books, 2018) 35.

2. Ibid. 137.

3. Lewis, C.S., *Mere Christianity* (Harper Collins, 2001) 98.

4. Pearcey, Nancy R., *Love Thy Body: Answering Hard Questions About Life and Sexuality* (Baker Books, 2018) 35.

5. Allberry, Sam, *What God Has to Say About Our Bodies: How the Gospel is Good News for Our Physical Selves* (Crossway, 2021) 98.

6. Westminster Theological Seminary, "Heidelberg Catechism," accessed June 1, 2023, https://students.wts.edu/resources/creeds/heidelberg.html.

7. Allberry, Sam, *What God Has to Say About Our Bodies: How the Gospel is Good News for Our Physical Selves* (Crossway, 2021) 138.

8. Bible Hub, "Ellicott's Commentary for English Readers: Romans 12:1," accessed March, 2023, https://biblehub.com/commentaries/ellicott/romans/12.htm.

Chapter 9

1. Keller, Timothy, "The Bible and Same Sex Relationships: A Review Article," *Redeemer Churches and Ministries*, 2015, https://www.redeemer.com/redeemer-report/article/the_bible_and_same_sex_relationships_a_review_article.

2. "Child Sex Abuse & Trafficking," Child USA: The Think Tank for Child Protection, accessed April 2023, https://childusa.org/child-sex-abuse.

3. Pearcey, Nancy R., *Love Thy Body: Answering Hard Questions About Life and Sexuality* (Baker Books, 2018) 11.

4. O'Mary, Lisa, "U.S. STD Cases Totaled 2.5 Million in Pandemic's Second Year." *WebMD*, March 16, 2023, https://www.webmd.com/sexual-conditions/news/20230316/us-std-cases-pandemic-second-year.

5. Mandel, Bethany, "New Study on 'Rise' in Transgenderism Shows It's a Fad, Especially Among Young Girls," *New York Post*, June 28, 2023, https://nypost.com/2023/06/28/new-study-on-rise-in-transgender-shows-its-a-fad-especially-among-young-girls/.

6. Sanger-Katz, Margot and Miller, Claire Cain and Bui, Quoctrung, "Who Gets Abortions in America?" *The New York Times*, December 14, 2021, https://www.nytimes.com/interactive/2021/12/14/upshot/who-gets-abortions-in-america.html.

7. Hauser, Christine, "How the Ohio Train Derailment and Its Aftermath Unfolded," *The New York Times*, May 31, 2023, https://www.nytimes.com/article/ohio-train-derailment-timeline.html.

8. Wikipedia: The Free Encyclopedia, "Pretty Woman," last modified May 19, 2023, https://en.wikipedia.org/wiki/Pretty_Woman.

9. Allberry, Sam, *Why Does God Care Who I Sleep With?* (The Good Book Company, 2020) 136.

10. McLaughlin, Rebecca, *The Secular Creed: Engaging Five Contemporary Claims* (The Gospel Coalition, 2021) 35.

11. Keller, Timothy, *The Meaning of Marriage: Facing the Complexities of Commitment with the Wisdom of God* (Penguin Books, 2011) 255–256.

12. Hellerman, Joseph H., *When the Church Was a Family: Recapturing Jesus' Vision for Authentic Christian Community* (B&H Academic, 2009) 35–38.

13. Slattery, Juli, *Rethinking Sexuality: God's Design and Why It Matters* (Multnomah, 2018) 55–56.

14. West, Christopher, *Theology of the Body for Beginners: A Basic Introduction to Pope John Paul II's Sexual Revolution* (Ascension, 2004) 30.

15. Allberry, Sam, "How Both Singleness and Marriage Testify to the Gospel," *Crossway Blog*, March 10, 2019, https://www.crossway.org/articles/how-both-singleness-and-marriage-testify-to-the-gospel.

Chapter 10

1. Lewis, C.S., *The Screwtape Letters* (Macmillan Publishing Co., 1961) 3.

2. Gombis, Timothy G., *The Drama of Ephesians: Participating in the Triumph of God* (InterVarsity Press, 2010) 159.

3. "Spiritual Warfare," Gospel in Life Podcast, July 3, 2012, https://podcast.gospelinlife.com/e/spiritual-warfare-1562113890.

4. Duguid, Iain M., *The Whole Armor of God: How Christ's Victory Strengthens Us for Spiritual Warfare* (Crossway, 2019) 17.

5. "John Piper, Tim Keller and Richard Coekin Talk About Ephesians," The Good Book Company, July 7, 2015, YouTube video, 1:35, https://www.youtube.com/watch?v=aCUf3daybzw.

6. Lavoie, Amy, "Ulrich explains that well-behaved women should make history," *The Harvard Gazette*, September 20, 2007, https://news.harvard.edu/gazette/story/2007/09/ulrich-explains-that-well-behaved-women-should-make-history.

More books from 10Publishing

Resources that point to Jesus